The Cry
of the Gull

The Cry
of the Gull

Emmanuelle Laborit

Translated by
Constantina Mitchell and
Paul Raymond Côté

GALLAUDET UNIVERSITY PRESS
Washington, D.C.

Gallaudet University Press
Washington, DC 20002

Originally published as *Le Cri de la Mouette,* © 1994 by
Editions Robert Laffont, S. A., Paris, France

Printed in the United States of America

Unless otherwise indicated, all photos are
from the author's personal collection.

Library of Congress Cataloging-in-Publication Data

Laborit, Emmanuelle
    [Cri de la mouette. English]
    The cry of the gull / Emmanuelle Laborit ; translated by
    Constantina Mitchell and Paul Raymond Côté.
        p.   cm.
    ISBN 1-56368-072-6 (alk. paper)
    1. Laborit, Emmanuelle.   2. Actors—France—Biography.
3. Deaf—France—Biography.   I. Title.
PN2638.L22A313   1998
792'.028'092—dc21
[b]   98-8775
                                                                  CIP

♾ The paper used in this publication meets the minimum
requirements of American National Standard for Information
Sciences—Permanence of Paper for Printed Library Materials,
ANSI Z39.48-198

Contents

Translators'
Acknowledgment

The translators wish to thank Harry Markowicz and Bernard Mottez (who were both instrumental in arranging the training session at Gallaudet University described in chapter nine of this book) and Alain Bernard for their help in clarifying certain factual information.

Chapter *1*

Secrets

Words have struck me as odd ever since I was a child. I use the term *odd* because of the strangeness I initially saw in them. What did all those funny expressions on the faces of people around me mean? Their mouths were rounded or stretched in all sorts of grimaces. Their lips were twisted in weird shapes. I could *feel* something different when people were angry, sad, or happy, but an invisible barrier separated me from the sounds that corresponded to their facial expressions. It seemed like both a transparent sheet of glass and a concrete wall. My movements were confined to one side and theirs to the other. And when I tried to ape their expressions, I could only form letters, never words. Sometimes they taught me one-syllable words or words made up of two identical syllables like *papa* and *mama*.

The simplest of concepts were even more mysterious. *Yesterday, tomorrow, today*. My mind worked in the present. What did *past* and *future* mean?

I took a giant leap forward when, with the help of sign language, I understood that *yesterday* was behind me and *tomorrow* in front of me. That was huge progress. Hearing people can hardly imagine what it's like because they're used to having words and concepts endlessly repeated to them from infancy. They come to understand them without even being aware of it.

Later, I realized that other words referred to people. *Emmanuelle* was me. *Papa* was him. *Mama* was her. *Marie* was my sister. I was Emmanuelle, an individual. I had a name, therefore I existed.

As soon as I understood that I was somebody, as soon as I realized that I was a living being, I was able to say "I." Before that, I always used *she* to mean myself. I was searching for my place in the world, for who I was and why I existed. And I found myself. My name is Emmanuelle Laborit.

Next, I was gradually able to analyze the link between actions and the words that described them, the connection between people and what they did. Suddenly the world was mine and I was part of it.

I was seven years old. I had just been born and come of age in one fell swoop.

My hunger and thirst for understanding the world, for learning and knowing about it, were tremendous. And my desire for learning is just as strong today as it was then. I learned to read and write French, my other language. I became talkative and asked questions about everything, but expressed myself sort of the way a bilingual foreigner would. Like most people, I finished secondary school. The written exams scared me more than the orals. That might seem strange coming from someone who has difficulty pronouncing words, but writing is even harder for me.

When I got the idea to write this book, some people told me I would never be able to do it. But that wasn't the case! When I decide to do something, I see it through to the end. I wanted to do it and I was going to. So I started working on my own creative endeavor with my usual determination.

Other people, the ones who were more intrigued by my project, wanted to know if I planned to do the writing myself or tell my story in sign language to a hearing person who would transcribe it.

I did both. In the process, written and signed words became like siblings, and sometimes twins.

My French is a bit stilted, like an acquired foreign language detached from its culture. Sign language is my real culture. French has the advantage of rendering what I want to express objectively. But my sensitivity, my poetry, my inner being, my true style all come through in the spatial word-dance of sign. Blending the two languages has made it possible for me to recount my young life in these few pages, from *yesterday* (when I was behind that concrete yet transparent barrier) to *today* (now that I've scaled the wall). A book is an important testimonial. It goes everywhere. It passes from hand to hand and mind to mind, and always leaves its mark. It's a means of communication rarely used by deaf people. My book will be the first of its kind in France, just as I was the first deaf actress to receive a Molière award for my work in the theater.

This book is one of life's gifts. It will let me say to both deaf and hearing people what I've always held back. It has a message and takes a position in the battle over sign language—an issue that continues to polarize many. I'm using my second language, the language of hearing people, to proclaim with absolute certainty that sign language is the native language of deaf people, our very own, the one that makes us "communicating" human beings. I want to say, too, that the deaf should be given access to everything. When it comes to languages, there can be no ghettos, no ostracism: all languages are valid in the pursuit of LIFE.

Chapter 2

Cry of the Seagull

I let out screams, lots of them, real ones. Not because I was hungry or thirsty, afraid, or in pain, but because I was beginning to want to talk. I wanted to hear myself, but the sounds I was making weren't rebounding back to me.

I could feel the vibrations. I knew I was screaming but the sounds didn't mean a thing to my mother and father. To them, they were like the piercing cries of a sea bird, like a gull gliding over the ocean. So they nicknamed me Mouette, which means *seagull* in French.

The little seagull shrieked above an ocean of noises she couldn't hear, and no one understood her cries.

"You were a very beautiful baby," my mother recalls. "It was an easy birth. You weighed 7 pounds 11 ounces. You cried when you were hungry. You laughed and babbled like other babies. You were happy. We didn't realize right away. We just thought you were well-behaved because, on evenings when we had friends over, you'd sleep soundly even with the music blaring in the living room, which was next to the room where you were sleeping. We were proud to have such a good baby. We thought you were 'normal' because you'd turn your head whenever a door slammed. We didn't know it was because you could feel the vibrations and drafts on the floor where you were playing. And when your father put on a record, you'd dance in your playpen, swaying back and forth, swinging your arms and legs."

I was at the age when babies crawl around on all fours and start trying to say "mama" and "dada." But I wasn't saying anything. I sensed vibrations on the floor. I felt them from the music and would join in with my seagull-like sounds. At least that's what I've been told.

I was a perceptive little seagull. I had a secret. A world all to myself.

I come from a seafaring family. My mother's father, grandfather, and brother were among the last of the Cape Horn sailors. That's another reason why they called me their little seagull. But the French words for "seagull" and "mute" look and sound practically the same: *mouette/muette*. So which was I? Today, that strange phonetic similarity makes me smile.

Uncle Fifou, my father's older brother, was the first to say, "Emmanuelle makes shrieking sounds because she can't hear herself." My father claims it was my uncle who "was the first to arouse our suspicions." "The scene is frozen in my mind," says my mother.

My parents didn't want to believe it. To such an extent, in fact, that it was only much later that I found out my paternal grandparents had been married in the chapel of the National Institute for the Deaf in Bordeaux. What's more, the institute's director was my grandmother's stepfather. In an attempt to hide their concern, perhaps, or avoid facing the truth, my parents had forgotten about all that! Basically, they were proud of not having a little brat who would wake them up in the wee hours of the morning. So they got into the habit of jokingly referring to me as their little seagull. It was their way of not admitting they were worried because I was different.

Some people say we end up yelling out what we really want kept silent. In my case, I had to yell to try to hear the difference between my screams and silence, to compensate for the absence of all the words I saw moving on my mother's and father's lips and whose meaning escaped me. And since my parents silenced their anguish, maybe I had to scream for them as well. Who knows?

"The pediatrician thought I was crazy," my mother says. "He didn't believe it either because you seemed to react normally to sounds, but it was the same old story—you were really just feeling vibrations. Yet when we clapped our hands next to you or behind you, you didn't turn your head in the direction of the noise. You didn't respond when you were called. And I could tell it wasn't normal. When I used to walk up to you, you seemed so surprised you would practically jump, as though you had become aware of my presence only a split second before. I started thinking

I had psychological problems, especially since the pediatrician still didn't want to believe me even though he saw you for checkups once a month.

"I set up yet another appointment with him to discuss my concerns. That's when he bluntly told me, 'Madam, I strongly suggest you get counseling!' Then, he slammed the door on purpose and since you just happened to turn around, maybe because you had felt the vibrations or simply because you found his behavior strange, he said, 'You can clearly see the idea's absurd!'

"I'm angry at him, and at myself for having believed him. After that office visit, your father and I went through a period of real anguish. We observed you constantly. We whistled, called you, slammed doors, watched you clap your hands and sway as though you were dancing to the music. One minute we believed you could hear, the next minute we thought you couldn't. We were totally confused.

"When you were nine months old, I took you to a specialist. He lost no time in telling me you had been born profoundly deaf. It was a tremendous shock. I couldn't accept it and neither could your father. We kept telling ourselves, 'It's a misdiagnosis. There's no way.' We went to see another specialist. I was so hoping he'd grin, reassure us, and send us home.

"Then we went to Trousseau Hospital with your father. During the examination, they made you listen to sounds so loud they practically pierced my eardrums. But you were totally unresponsive to them. You were sitting on my lap and that's when I realized it was true. I asked the specialist three questions.

'Will she talk?'

'Yes but it'll take a long time.'

'What should we do?'

'Have her fitted with a hearing aid and get her into speech therapy as soon as possible. Avoid sign language at all costs.'

'Is there any way I could meet some deaf adults?'

'That wouldn't be a good idea. They belong to a generation that didn't have early training. You'd be disappointed and discouraged.'

"Your father was completely overcome. I cried. Where had this 'curse' come from? Was it genetic? Had it been caused by an illness during pregnancy? I felt guilty and so did your father. We tried, to no avail, to find out who might have been deaf on one side of the family or the other."

I can understand the shock my parents suffered from all that. Parents of deaf children always want to assign guilt. They're always looking for the guilty party. But blaming one parent or the other for a child's deafness is horrible for the child. It shouldn't happen. They still don't know why I'm deaf and never will and it's probably better that way.

My mother says she didn't know what to do with me. She would look at me but couldn't come up with any activities to create a bond between us. Sometimes she couldn't even bring herself to play with me. She stopped talking to me. What was going through her head was, "I can't even tell her I love her any more because she can't hear."

She was in a state of shock, stunned. She couldn't think rationally.

I have strange memories of my early childhood. It's just chaos in my head, a series of completely unrelated images, like film sequences edited together with long strips of blank film, giant lost spaces.

My life up to age seven is full of gaps. I only have visual memories, like flashbacks, images whose time-frame I can't place. I believe there was no sense whatsoever of time progression in my mind during that period. Past, future, everything was on the same time-space line. Mother would say *yesterday,* but I didn't understand where or what *yesterday* was. *Tomorrow* had no meaning either. And I couldn't ask what they meant. I was helpless, completely unaware of time passing. There was daylight and the darkness of night, and that was it.

I still can't assign dates to things during the period from my birth to age seven, or arrange what I did in chronological order. Time was in a holding pattern. I just experienced things as they happened. Maybe there are memories buried in my head, but I don't know in what order they happened or how old I was. I can't place them. As for events—or I should say situations or scenes because everything was visual—I lived each as an isolated experience, in the present. That's why, in trying to reassemble the puzzle of my early childhood so I could write about it, I found only fragments of images.

Other perceptions dwell in a turmoil that is out of memory's reach. They're locked in that period of solitude, behind that wall of silence, when words were mysterious and language was absent. And yet I was able to manage. I don't know how, but I did.

"Sitting up in your bed," my mother tells me, "you'd see me disappear and come back, to your amazement. You didn't know where I'd gone. To the kitchen, perhaps. I was two distinct images, Mommy disappearing and Mommy coming back. And there was no link between the two."

Chapter 3

Dolls Don't Talk

I started learning how to communicate with a speech therapist, using the Borel-Maisonny method. She was an extraordinary woman who was receptive to my mother's tale of woe and put up with her anger and tears. She played dolls and water games with me, and we had tea parties. She showed my mother it was possible to have a relationship with me, to make me laugh, so I could go on living as I had before she knew about my deafness.

I learned to pronounce the letters of the alphabet. They taught me the letters using mouth movements and hand gestures.

My mother sat in on the sessions, which ultimately became a way for her to assume her maternal role. By identifying with the therapist, my mother learned to talk to me again. Our way of communicating was instinctive, animal-like. What I call "umbilical." It revolved around simple things like eating, drinking, and sleeping. My mother didn't stop me from gesturing. She didn't have the heart to, even though that's what they recommended. We also had signs that were our very own, completely made up.

"You tried everything under the sun to communicate with me," my mother remembers, "and it made me laugh so hard it brought tears to my eyes! I'd turn your face towards mine so you could try to make out simple words, and you'd imitate me as I went along. It was so cute."

I don't know how many times she drew my face close to hers in a mother-child encounter that was both fascinating and terrifying, and that functioned as our language.

From that moment on, there was hardly any room left for my father. It was even harder when he came home from work. I wasn't spending much time with him and we didn't have an "umbilical" code. I would utter a few words but he almost never understood. It hurt him to see my mother communicating with me in a language whose intimacy was beyond his reach. He felt excluded. And naturally he was, because it wasn't a language that could be shared by all three of us, or with anyone else. He wanted to communicate directly with me and being excluded bothered him. When he came home in the evening, we had nothing to say to each other. I often went up to my mother and pulled on her arm for her to tell me what he was saying. I wanted so much to "talk" with him and know more about him.

I started saying a few words. Like all deaf children, I wore a hearing aid and more or less put up with it. It channeled noises into my head but they were all the same. It was impossible to differentiate between them or use them in any way. It was more tiring than anything else. But the therapists said I had to wear it! I don't know how many times the ear piece fell into my soup. My mother says the family would find consolation in trite statements like:

"She may be deaf but she's so cute!"

"She'll just be that much smarter!"

FLASHBACK:

I have a fabulous doll collection. I'm not sure how many, but dolls I have! How old am I? I don't know, but I'm at the doll age. It's my doll phase. When it's time to go to sleep, I have to arrange them so they're all lined up in a row. I tuck them in. Their hands have to be outside the covers. Then I close their eyes. I spend a long time arranging them before I go to bed. I probably talk to them. I'm sure I do, using the same code as with my mother, making the sign for sleep. Once all the doll people are in bed, I can go to bed, too.

It's strange that I arranged my dolls so methodically while everything in my head was completely muddled, vague, and mixed-up. I'm still trying to figure out why I used to do it, why I spent an eternity arranging my dolls. My parents always hurried me along so they could put me to bed.

It got on my father's nerves. It got on everybody's nerves. But I couldn't sleep if my dolls weren't all in place. They had to be perfectly lined up, eyes closed, the blanket pulled up exactly to where it should be with their arms on top. It all had to be fiendishly precise even though everything in my head was disorganized. Maybe it was my way of putting all the mixed-up experiences I'd had during the day in order before going to sleep. Maybe I was going through the motions of tidying up the day's disorder. During the day, my life was total disorder. At night, I slept neatly tucked away like my dolls, in complete quiet. Dolls don't talk.

I lived in silence because I wasn't communicating. I guess that's what real silence must be like—the total darkness of what can't be communicated. Everyone was dark silence for me except my parents, especially my mother.

Silence therefore had a special meaning for me—the absence of communication. But from another perspective, I've never lived in complete silence. I have my own noises that are inexplicable to hearing people. I have my imagination and it has its noises in image form. I imagine sounds in terms of colors. My own personal silence has colors. It's never black and white.

I perceive hearing people's noises in images too, as sensations. The tranquil waves that gently roll up on the beach evoke a sensation of serenity and calm. Waves that bristle and gallop while arching their backs evoke anger. The wind means my hair floating in the air, freshness and softness on my skin.

Light was important. I liked the day, not the night.

I used to sleep on a sofa in the living room of my parents' tiny apartment. My father was a medical student and my mother, a school teacher. She took time off from her studies to raise me. We weren't very rich, and the apartment was small. I was unaware of all that since I had no idea at the time how society and the hearing world were structured. At night, I slept alone on the sofa. I can still see that yellow and orange sofa. I see a brown wooden table. I see the dining room table with its white frame. The sounds I imagined were always linked to colors, but I couldn't say that a specific sound was blue, green, or red. It's that colors and light played a part in the way I imagined sounds and perceived every situation.

In the light, I could monitor everything with my eyes. Darkness was synonymous with non-communication and, therefore, silence. Absence of light meant panic. Later on, I didn't mind turning out the light before going to sleep.

I have a memory about the darkness of night and how it affected me when I was little: I'm in the living room, lying on my bed, and I see the reflection of headlights shining through the window onto the wall. All those lights that keep coming and going frighten me. I still see them in my mind. There's no wall between the living room and my parents' room. It's a big open space with no door. There's an armchair, a bed, and the large cushion-covered sofa where I sleep. I see myself there as a child, but I don't know how old I am. I'm scared. I was always scared of the cars' headlights at night, those images that came and went on the wall.

Sometimes my parents would tell me they were going out. But did I actually understand what "going out" meant? I thought I was being abandoned, deserted. My perception was that my parents disappeared and then reappeared. Were they going to reappear, though? And when? The notion of "when" was unknown to me. I didn't have the words to express my apprehension to them. I didn't have a language. I couldn't tell them. It was horrible.

I think I could probably guess from their nervous behavior that they were going to "disappear," but their departure always ended up taking me by surprise because I became conscious of it at night. They fed me dinner, put me to bed, and waited till I was sound asleep. They thought they could leave and I wouldn't know. But I would wake up all alone. Maybe I'd wake up because they had left. And I was afraid of the ghostly headlights on the wall.

I was incapable of expressing or explaining that fear. My parents must have thought that nothing could wake me up since I was deaf! But the lights were strange, scary night sounds to me and they alarmed me tremendously. If I had been able to make myself understood, my parents wouldn't have left me all alone. A deaf child has to have somebody there at night. Has to.

I can recall a nightmare I had, too: I'm in the backseat of a car and my mother is driving. I call out to her. I want to ask her something. I want her to answer me. I call her but she doesn't turn around. I keep on calling, and when she finally turns to answer me, we have an accident. The car ends up in a ravine and then in the ocean. I see water all around me. It's horrible. Unbearable. The accident is my fault and I wake up in a state of complete anxiety.

I used to call out to my mother all day long so we could talk. I always wanted to know what was going on, to be in on things. It was a genuine need. She was the only one who truly understood me because of the language we had invented together—that animal-like, "umbilical" language, our special, instinctive code, comprised of mime and gestures. I needed her all the time because there were so many things all mixed-up in my head, so many questions. My great apprehension at that age was crystallized in that nightmare where she didn't turn to look at me.

It's different for children who learn sign language when they're very young or who have deaf parents. They make remarkable strides. I'm astounded by their development. I was really behind because I only learned to sign at seven. Before then I must have been a little like a "retard" or a wild animal.

Now that I look back, I find it incredible. How did I manage before I knew how to sign? I didn't have a language. How could I develop as an individual? How did I understand things? Get people's attention? Ask for things? I remember gesturing a lot.

Was I capable of thinking? Of course, but what did I think about? About my inexhaustible desire to truly communicate. About the sensation I had of being locked behind a huge door that I couldn't open to make people understand me.

I tugged at my mother's sleeve or dress. I pointed to objects, tons of things. She would understand and answer me.

I was slowly making headway and starting to imitate words. *Water*, for example, was the first word I learned to pronounce. I copied what I saw on my mother's lips. I couldn't hear myself, but I rounded my lips to make the sound. The vibrations I felt in my throat created a distinct sound for my mother. And so these words became special for her and me, words that no one else could understand. Mother wanted me to force myself to speak, and I tried for her sake, but what I really wanted to do was point and show. When I had to go to the bathroom, I would point in that direction. To eat, I pointed to the food I wanted and then put my hand to my mouth.

Before I was seven, there were no words, no sentences in my head. Only images. When I tugged at my mother to tell her something, I didn't want her to look away, but rather at me. She should be looking at my face and nothing else. I remember that. That means I was capable of thinking; I was "thinking" communication. And I wanted it.

I remember some unusual situations. Family get-togethers, for example, when there were loads of people around. Their mouths moved a lot and it all bored me. I would go into another room and look at objects, things. I'd pick them up to really look at them. Then I'd go back to the room full of people and tug at my mother. Tugging at her was my way of calling her so she'd look at me and pay attention to me. It was hard when there were people around. I lost contact with her. I was alone on my planet and I wanted her to come back. She was my only link with the world. My father would look at us. He still didn't understand a thing.

I can remember seeing him very angry, with a particular expression on his face. I imitated his anger as if to ask, "Is something wrong?"

Then he would say, "No, no. It's okay!"

Sometimes I used to go tug at my mother so she could translate because I wanted to know more. I wanted to know what was going on. Why, why had I seen anger on my father's face? But she couldn't translate all the time. When she couldn't, I was left in dark silence.

When there were people around, I stared at their faces. I observed all their facial tics and quirks. Some people didn't look at the person they were talking to at the dinner table. They played with their place setting or ran their fingers through their hair. They just looked like images doing things. I couldn't say what I felt. But I could see. I saw if they were happy or not. I saw if they were irritated or if they weren't listening. I had my eyes for listening, but that was not enough. I could see they were using their mouths to communicate with each other. "That must be how I'm different. They make noise with their mouths," I thought. I didn't know what noise was, or silence for that matter. The two words didn't have any meaning.

But it wasn't really silent inside me. I could hear very high-pitched whistling sounds. I used to think they were coming from somewhere else, from outside me. But no. They were my noises. I was the only one who heard them. Was I noise on the inside and silence on the outside?

They must have fitted me with a hearing aid at nine months. Little deaf children often have hearing aids with two earphones connected by a cord in the shape of a **Y** and a microphone on their stomach. It's a monophonic device. I don't remember hearing things with it. Noises maybe. But they were noises that I heard anyway, like vibrations from cars going by or music. The device made them unbearably loud. But could I hear the sounds children hear? No, my toys were mute.

The noises were too loud. They had no meaning. They brought me nothing and just tired me out. I used to take my hearing aid off to sleep because the noise made me nervous. Loud, nameless, disconnected noises were stressful.

"The speech therapist told us not to worry," my mother remembers. "They said you would eventually be able to speak. They gave us hope. With speech therapy and hearing aids you'd become 'hearing.' Of course you'd be behind for your age, but you'd manage. Although it was completely illogical, we hoped that you would end up actually being able to hear someday, as if by magic. It was so hard to accept the fact that you had been born into a world that was different from ours."

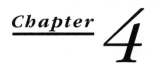

Chapter 4

Stomachs and Music

After they fitted me with a hearing aid, I began to make the distinction between hearing and deaf people (but I'm not sure exactly when). Hearing people simply didn't wear hearing aids. There were those with and those without. It was a simple distinction.

I wanted to say things, lots of things, but that wall was still there. And it saddened me. I could see that my mother and father were sad, too. I really felt sadness, but wanted my parents to smile and be cheerful. I wanted to make them happy. But I didn't know how. I asked myself, "What's wrong with me? Why do I make them sad?" I still hadn't understood that I was deaf. I only knew I was different.

My first recollection? I have no first or last childhood memory because of the disorganization of my mind at that time. There were only sensations, and eyes and a body to take in those sensations.

I remember stomachs.

FLASHBACK:

My mother is pregnant with my little sister and I feel the vibrations very strongly. I sense that something's happening. With my face buried in my mother's belly, I can "hear" life. I have trouble imagining there's a baby in Mommy's tummy. That seems impossible to me. I see a person. And there's supposed to be another person inside of that same person? I say it isn't true. It's a joke. But I like my mother's belly and the sound of life inside it.

I also like my father's stomach, in the evening when he's discussing things with friends or my mother. When I'm tired, I lie down beside him with my head on his stomach, and I can feel his voice. It goes through his stomach and I can feel the vibrations. It soothes and reassures me. It's like a lullaby. I fall asleep to the vibrations, like a nursery rhyme in my head.

My perception of conflict was physical, too, but it was different: My mother is giving me a spanking. She goes away afterwards. Her hands are sore and so is my behind. Both of us are crying. I can still remember that spanking. I must have understood why she was spanking me, but I don't remember now. My parents never hit me, so I think she was really mad. But I don't know why. That's my only recollection of being punished.

Conflicts with my mother could get complicated. For example, when I didn't want to eat something, Mother would say, "You have to finish your plate."

"I don't want to."

So she plays airplane with the tiny spoon. A spoonful for Daddy, one for Grandma . . . I see what her game is . . . a spoonful for me. I open my mouth and swallow. But sometimes I don't want to eat. Period. I tell Mommy off. The little seagull is angry. And when I'm tired of it all, I leave the table. They all think I'm joking, but I'm not. I'm really mad and want to leave. I pack my suitcase with my dolls.

It's a doll's suitcase, so I don't put my coat in it. I put the doll's coats in along with the dolls. I don't know why. Maybe because the dolls are me and I want to show that I'm the one leaving. I go out to the street. My mother panics and comes after me. That's what I do when we argue and I'm really mad. I'm a person, too. I can't always obey. I'm always supposed to agree with my mother, but I want to be independent. Emmanuelle is different. Mommy and I are different from each other.

My father and I used to play together. We had fun and laughed a lot, but I don't know if we were really communicating. Neither did he at the time. And he felt bad about that. As soon as he found out I was deaf, the first thing he wondered was how I would ever hear music. When I was very little, he took me to concerts as a way of passing his love of music on to me. Or maybe he was refusing to face the fact that I was deaf. Anyway, I thought it was fantastic. And it's still fantastic that he didn't put up a barrier between music and me. I was happy to be with him. And I'm convinced I perceived the music intensely. Not with my ears, but with my body. For a long time my father harbored the hope that I would one day wake up, as if from a long sleep. Like Sleeping Beauty. He was sure that music would work that magic. Since he was wild about all kinds of music—classical, jazz, the Beatles—and since I'd always sway to the beat, my father took me to concerts. I grew up believing I could share everything with him.

One evening, my Uncle Fifou, who was a musician, was playing the guitar. I can see him now. The image is clear in my mind. The whole family is listening. He wants to make me experience the guitar, so he tells me to bite the neck of the instrument. As I do, he begins to play. I keep on biting for hours. I can feel every vibration in my body, both high and low notes. The music enters my body and takes up residence there. It begins to play inside me. Mother looks at me completely astounded. She tries to do the same thing but doesn't like it. She says it echoes in her head. To this day my uncle's guitar still bears my teeth marks.

I was lucky to have music when I was a child. Some parents of deaf children think it's pointless, so they deprive their children of music. And some deaf children make fun of music. I love it. I feel its vibrations. The visual spectacle of the concert has an impact on me, too. The people in the concert hall, the lighting effects, the atmosphere are all part of the vibrations. I can sense that everybody's gathered together at the concert for the same thing. It's fantastic: the sparkling golden saxophone, the trumpet players with their cheeks puffed out, the basses. I feel with my feet, or my whole body if I'm stretched out on the floor. And I can imagine the sounds. I've always imagined them. I perceive music through my body, with my bare feet on the floor, latching onto the vibrations. The piano, electric guitar, African drums, percussion instruments, all have colors and I sway along with them. That's how I see it, in color. But the difference between the guitar and the violin is hard for me to recognize. I can't get the violin. I can't feel it with my feet. The violin flies away. It must be high-pitched, like a bird. Like a bird's song, it's uncatchable. Its music is upward, reaching for the sky, not down towards the earth. Sounds in the air must be high; sounds at earth level, low-pitched. The tom-tom makes music that comes up from the earth. I just love African music. I feel it with my feet, my head, my whole body. But I have trouble with classical music. It's so high in the air I can't catch it.

Music is a rainbow of vibrant colors. It's a language beyond words. It's universal. The most beautiful form of art that exists. It's capable of making the human body physically vibrate. Suppose I came from another planet and ran into humans all speaking different languages. I'm sure I would be able to understand them because I'd sense what they were feeling. That's what happens with music. Notes begin to dance inside my body like flames in a fireplace. The fire sets the rhythm: small, big, small, faster, slower— vibrations, emotions, and colors swirl to a magical beat. The field of music is very wide. It's immense and I often get lost in it.

The sound of singing voices remains a mystery to me. Just once, the mystery was broken. I don't know how old I was, but I was still living only in the present.

FLASHBACK:
Maria Callas is on TV. My parents are watching and I'm sitting with them in front of the set. I see a powerful-looking woman. She seems to have a strong personality. Suddenly, there's a close-up and at that moment I feel her voice. As I stare at her intently, I realize what her voice must be like. I get the impression that the song she's singing isn't a very happy one. I see that her voice is coming from deep within, from far away, that she's singing from her stomach, from her guts. It has a tremendous effect on me.

Did I really hear her voice? I have no idea. But I truly felt emotion. Nothing like that ever happened, before or after. Maria Callas had touched me. That's the only time in my life that I felt or imagined a voice singing.

Other singers leave me cold. When I watch video clips of them on TV, I sense a lot of violence, lots of images, one after the other. It's impossible to understand anything. They're all so fast, I can't even begin to imagine the music that goes along with them. But the words of some singers like Carole Laure, Jacques Brel, and Jean-Jacques Goldman really move me.

And then there's Michael Jackson! When I see him dance, it looks like he has an electric body. The beat is electrifying. I associate it with an electric image. I feel the electricity.

Dance is something that permeates your body. When I was a teenager, I used to like to go to nightclubs with my deaf friends. It was the only place where the music could be blaring full-blast and not bother anybody. I danced all night with my body pressed against the wall, swaying to the rhythm. The others (the hearing people there) looked at me in astonishment. They must have thought I was crazy.

Chapter 5

White Cat, Black Cat

My father used to take me to kindergarten. I liked going with him, but when I got there I would always end up alone in a corner, drawing. In the evening, my mother and I would draw some more. I loved it when she drew a picture and I was supposed to add an eye or a nose. There were drawings everywhere. We used to play a game called Battle, too. Each player had a special color.

I also remember a room with a strange revolving disc. We would put a piece of paper on it, then my mother and I would spurt different colors of paint onto the paper. The colors spread out randomly with the speed of the disc. I didn't know how it worked but it was beautiful.

Another thing we did was watch cartoons on TV or at the movies. After fifteen minutes of Tweety and Sylvester, I was crying, sniveling, and gasping so much my mother got worried. I saw the other kids laughing at Sylvester's blunders, but couldn't figure out why they thought it was funny. It was cruel and it made me feel bad. It wasn't fair that Sylvester always got caught and flattened up against a wall. That's how I saw it. Maybe I was too sensitive. Besides, I really liked cats.

I had a white cat. As far as I knew, it didn't have a name but I was so glad to have it. I used to make it jump in the air and play airplane with it. I'd play helicopter with it and pull it by the tail. I'm sure it was hell for the cat, but it loved me just the same. I did nothing but badger it and it still loved me!

One day, we found the cat with its stomach split open. I don't know how or when it happened. We were in the country. My father was a medical student at the time and tried to save it by sewing its stomach back up.

But the operation failed and the cat died. I asked what had happened and my father said, "It's over." For me that meant the cat had disappeared. It was gone. I wouldn't see it any more.

I didn't know the meaning of death. For days I asked where the cat was. They kept explaining that it was over and that I'd never ever see it again. I didn't understand *never,* or *dead.* All I understood was that *dead* meant it was over, *finished.* I thought big people were immortal. They went away and came back. Therefore, they would never be finished.

But it wasn't the same for me. I was going to "go away" like the cat. I couldn't see myself growing up. I thought I'd always be little, all my life. I thought I was limited to my present state. And above all, I thought I was unique, the only one like me in the world. Emmanuelle is deaf and no one else is. Emmanuelle is different. Emmanuelle will never grow up.

Since I couldn't communicate like other people, I couldn't be like them, like grown-ups who can hear. So I was going to be "finished." Sometimes it was impossible to communicate with people. I couldn't ask about all the things I wanted to know and understand. Or people just didn't answer me. That's when I thought about death. I was afraid, and now I know why: I had never seen a deaf adult. I had only seen deaf children in the special education class at my kindergarten. So, in my mind, deaf children never grew up. We were all going to die as little children. I even think I was unaware that hearing people had once been children! There was no possible point of reference for me.

When I saw that the cat wasn't around any more, that it had "gone away," I tried with all my might to understand what had happened. I really wanted to see the cat again, to understand. I wanted to see it because I could only understand things with my eyes. My parents didn't show me the dead cat so I was left with the idea of "gone away." It was all too confusing.

When my little sister was born, we got another cat. A black one this time. His name was Bobbin. My father chose the name, in deference to Freud's *Fort-Da,*[1] he said. The cat always used to play with bobbins of thread. He knew I was deaf, and I knew he knew. It was obvious. When

---

[1] Translators' note: Freud speaks of a case in which a child played a game that involved repeatedly spinning a bobbin to make it disappear (*fort*) and reappear (*da*). According to Freud, the child was unknowingly mastering his feelings of displeasure caused by his mother's absences.

Bobbin was hungry, he would follow my mother around and meow at her. He'd run circles around her. Naturally, she could hear him even though she couldn't see him. When we first got him, he tried that with me but soon realized I wasn't reacting and that ticked him off. So he'd plunk himself down right in front of my head and meow in my face. It was obvious: he knew that to be "heard" he had to stare with his beautiful green eyes deep into mine. Sometimes when I was lying on my bed, he would grab at my feet to play. I wanted to communicate with him and let him know he was being a pain. I tried using gestures to tell him, "Stop it, you're bugging me." But he didn't get the message. I knew when he was angry because he didn't respond. He turned into a sort of cat statue.

When I saw Tweety and Sylvester, and all the violence heaped on that poor cat, I hated Tweety. He teased Sylvester and never got flustered. The poor kitty didn't have a clue about what was going on and always took a beating. He may have been naive, but that Tweety was really rotten!

I was striving for a difficult kind of independence in a difficult world. I even had trouble pronouncing the word difficult. I used to say, "It's tifikul."

It was "tifikul" to say "tifikul."

It was "tifikul" for me to have an existence independent of my mother. I tried doing things without the help of my "umbilical cord." All alone, for a change of pace, as an adventure. I remember one instance in particular. How old was I? Was it before or after the cat died? I don't know, but I said, "I'm going to go to the bathroom by myself."

I didn't actually say that to my mother. I only said the words in my mind. Usually, when I had to go, I'd call my mother. But that time, we were at some friends' house and she was busy chatting. She wasn't paying attention to me, so I decided I was going to manage all alone.

I went into the bathroom and locked the door like a big person. But then I couldn't get out! I must have jammed the lock or done something to it. I began screaming and screaming and banging on the door. Being locked inside and not being able to get out was torture. My mother was on the other side of the door and could hear the banging. But of course I didn't know that. Suddenly all communication was cut off. There was literally a wall between my mother and me. It was frightening.

I'm sure my mother tried to reassure me. She probably said, "Don't worry, stay calm." But at the time, I couldn't hear her, since I couldn't see her. I thought she was still talking with her friend and that I was all alone. I was terrified. I thought I'd spend the rest of my life in that little room screaming in silence!

Finally I saw a piece of paper being slipped under the door. My mother had made a drawing, because I didn't know how to read yet. It was a picture of a child crying that had been crossed out. Next to it was a picture of a child laughing. I realized that she was on the other side of the door telling me to smile and that everything would be okay. But she didn't make a drawing to show that she would open the door. She was just telling me to laugh, and not cry. So I was still panic-stricken. I could feel myself screaming. I felt my vocal chords vibrating. When I let out high-pitched sounds, my vocal chords don't vibrate at all. But if I make low-pitched sounds, if I yell, I feel the vibrations. That day, I made my vocal chords vibrate till I was out of breath.

I must have cried a long time, like an angry seagull in a storm, before a locksmith came and opened the door, that wall separating me from my mother.

Chapter 6

It's "Tifikul"

Everything was difficult. What would have been the simplest of things for a hearing child was hard for me.

They put me in a mainstream kindergarten class for deaf children, and I started making friends with the other kids. That's actually where my social life began.

The speech therapist was able to get me to pronounce a few audible words. In the beginning, I expressed myself with my own particular blend of speech and gesture. "Up to the age of two," my mother says, "you went to a speech therapy center upstairs from a venereal disease clinic. That got me mad. Was deafness a disease to be ashamed of? Then we put you in the neighborhood kindergarten. One day when I came to get you, the teacher was telling the children stories to develop their language skills. You were sitting all by yourself, drawing at a table in a corner, completely oblivious to what was going on. You didn't look very happy."

I don't remember much about that phase of my life. I do remember, though, that I drew a lot. Drawings were important to me. They replaced communication. Through them, I could express part of the unanswered questions that filled my head. But as for that kindergarten with its so-called mainstream class, I've forgotten about it. Or rather, I'd like to forget about it. All those kids sitting in a circle around a teacher telling stories—is that really mainstreaming?

What was I doing there all alone sitting in front of my drawings or jumping rope on the playground? What were they teaching me? Nothing, as far as I'm concerned. What was the point? Who was benefiting from it?

I have a few mental images from that period of my life. One in particular stands out. My father came to get me when I was in the middle of washing my hands at the playground faucet. "Hurry up. We're leaving," he said.

I don't know how he said that or what he did to communicate the fact that I had to hurry so we could leave, but I felt it. He must have prodded me a bit. He probably looked rushed and anxious. Anyway, I got the message from his behavior: "We don't have much time." But I wanted to make him understand another message: "I haven't finished washing my hands." Then, all of a sudden, he wasn't there any more and I started crying my eyes out. There had been a misunderstanding. We hadn't understood each other. He was gone. He had vanished. And there I was all alone, crying. Was I crying about our misunderstanding or because I was alone? Or was it because he had disappeared? I think it was probably about the misunderstanding.

That scene is symbolic of the almost constant breakdown in communication between them and us, the hearing and the deaf. The only way I can understand a piece of information is by visualizing it. I think of it as a scene where I mix physical sensations with a sharpness of observation typical of a mime artist. If something is expressed quickly, it's hard for me to be sure I've understood. But I try to respond at the same pace. That day, when I was washing my hands at the faucet, my father hadn't understood what I wanted to say. Or maybe I was the one who hadn't understood him. And the penalty for that misunderstanding was that he left!

Naturally he came back to get me after a while. I have no idea how long it was, but I remember I was lonely and desperate. I couldn't explain the reason for my tears to him because everything used to get so complicated when there was a misunderstanding like that. Another situation would always ensue that was even harder to understand than the first.

I don't know if the strange scene I just described is a real memory or if I imagined it. In any case, it's strikingly symbolic of the difficulty I had communicating with my father at that time.

Tifikul is a child's word born of that difficulty. One day, when I must have been older, he and I were home alone. He was cooking steaks and wanted to know if I wanted mine well-done or rare. I could see he was trying to show me the difference between raw and cooked. He used the radiator to explain hot and cold. I understood hot and cold, but not raw and cooked. It went on for a long time, till finally he got mad and cooked both steaks the same.

Another time, he was watching a movie on TV. The name of one of the characters was Laborie, like ours except with an *e*. He kept trying to show me the difference between the *t* in our name and the *e* in the character's name on bits of paper. I just couldn't get it, and I kept telling him over and over, "It's tifikul. It's tifikul."

He didn't understand what I was trying to say. We were both exhausted, so we gave up and waited till my mother got home. He asked her what I meant and she burst out laughing, "It's difficult!"

But it was as "tifikul" for him as it was for me, and that was tough on him. Actually, it was tough on me, too. Deaf children are even more vulnerable and sensitive than others. I know I often used to swing back and forth between anger and laughter.

Anger, for example, would set in when nobody could be bothered to talk to me at mealtime. I would pound on the table furiously. I wanted to "talk," to understand what people were saying. I was sick and tired of being held prisoner of a silence they made no attempt to break. I was always trying hard, but they weren't doing enough. Hearing people didn't make much of an effort and I begrudged them that.

I remember one question that stuck in my mind: How did they understand each other with their backs turned? It was "tifikul" for me to realize that people could talk to each other even if they weren't face to face. I could only understand someone if we were both looking at each other. The only way I could get people's attention was by tugging at them—on a sleeve, the hem of a skirt, or a pant leg. That meant, "Look at me. Show me your face, your eyes, so I can understand you."

Seeing. If I couldn't see, I was lost. I needed the help of facial expressions and mouth movements.

I used my voice, too. I would call out to my father when he played the piano. I yelled "Daddy, Daddy" till he finally looked at me. But what did I want to tell him? I really don't know.

And I banged on things. I poked my mother and took her head in my hands to force her to look right at me.

When the doctor came, he would hunt for the spot where I hurt by poking me till I screamed. As a child, that was my way of talking to doctors when I was sick.

I did a lot of things on the sly. Basically, they were my little experiments.

I loved cough syrup. I secretly polished off every bottle I could find and then, of course, got sick. Nobody had told me cough syrup was bad. How could I know that? It was sweet. It tasted good. And it was supposed to make you better because the doctor prescribed it.

I loved "talami," too. That was my word for dried salami. It was like candy to me when I was little. I would steal it and hide it in the closet between piles of clothes or anywhere I could. But the smell of well-chewed bits always tipped my mother off.

When I was around five or six, I was going to school with deaf children and didn't feel isolated any more. The teacher knew I was deaf. I learned how to count with dominoes, and I learned the alphabet and how to paint. Now, going to school was fun.

I had a little deaf friend who came to my house to play. They would put us in a room together. Communicating was easier between us because we had our own signs and gestures.

We played with fire and candles because we weren't supposed to. I loved experimenting with whatever was off limits.

We watched *Goldorak* cartoons and then acted them out. We played with dolls, fought, and jumped around.

I spent a lot of time watching my parents and when I played, I tried recreating what I had seen. I was the mother in charge of the house, tea parties, and cooking. My little friend's job was to look after the children— the dolls. We pretended he was just coming home from work and then we playacted:

"Okay, you do this. I'll do that."

"No. I'll do it."

Then we would argue some more, and that's how the game went.

Understanding the difference between a man and a woman was also "tifikul." I could clearly see that my mother had breasts and my father didn't. My parents dressed differently. One was Mommy and one was Daddy. But besides that? I wanted to know the difference between my little friend and me, too.

Once, when we were on vacation in the south of France, he and I were playing in the water together. Since we were little, we weren't wearing bathing suits so the difference between him and me was apparent. I thought it was funny, and so simple. I understood. We were both deaf children, but we weren't completely identical.

I was like my mother, except that she could hear and I couldn't. She was a big person, but I would never get big. My little friend and I would soon be "finished." That was the period of my life when we still hadn't seen any deaf adults yet and so we couldn't imagine that you could grow up and be deaf, too. There was no point of reference or comparison to make us see that. So we were going to "leave" soon, be "finished"; in other words, die.

And I thought that when I died, my soul would pass into the body of another baby. But this time, the baby would be hearing. I can't explain that strange transformation. How did I know I had a soul? And, at that age, what did I mean by a soul?

I figured it out in my own way after watching a cartoon on TV. It was a story about a little girl. You didn't see her parents for a long time. So to me, that meant they had gone, just like the white cat. To leave was the same as to die. So I thought they were dead. Then the little girl found her parents again. Naturally, they were the same people as at the beginning of the story. It was just that she had been separated from them. But I concocted another story from it: Her parents had come back from the dead and entered other bodies. That's what I called a soul, "leaving and coming back." A soul was something you had or were, and that would leave and come back. In trying to understand death, I must have combined my white cat's disappearance and the cartoon.

At five or six, it's difficult enough for a hearing child to learn concepts. For me, the process was entirely dependent on visual images. The consequence was that I thought that when I was "finished," when it was my turn to leave along with my little friend, our souls would come back in the bodies of other babies. But those babies would be hearing. Maybe I thought the child who was going to take my place would be able to hear because being deaf made life hard for me. Because I didn't have a language to liberate me yet.

It's "tifikul" to understand the world, but you deal with it as best you can. I don't think asking my little friend to show me his private parts at the beach so I could tell the difference between mommies and daddies was much different from what hearing children do.

I believe the major distinguishing characteristic of the way I perceived things before I knew sign language hinged on two things: the absolute necessity of seeing something to be able to understand it, and, having seen it, the momentary impossibility of seeing it differently. That two possible situations might arise out of a single visual element was hard to fathom. For example, I love my maternal grandparents. Conversing with them wasn't easy, but they took care of me a lot when I was kindergarten age. And when I try to recall a visual memory of them, the first thing I see is a dog!

That's because the dog is linked to a situation that I associate with my grandparents and with having to understand a concept for which hearing people had two definitions but, in my mind, was wordless.

First situation: The dog is with his master. It's a big, friendly Doberman type, and they let me pet him.

Second situation: The dog's master is off at work and the dog is alone in a car. I walk up to the car and open the door. The dog barks in my face and bears his teeth at me. I'm terrified. Before, he let me pet him. Now he wants to bite me! I can't imagine two different types of behavior from the same animal image. In the first situation, no one explained the concepts of "friendly" and "vicious" as they related to dogs.

I sense danger. I run away and the dog darts after me. He bites me on the shoulder and I fall. My father comes running and the dog dashes off.

My father wants to give me a shot, but I don't want one. Needles terrify me. My mother realizes that I'm afraid of needles and does her best to comfort me. There they are, the two of them gesticulating above my head, one trying to give me a shot, the other reassuring me. The only thing I can gather from their discussion is the threat of that horrible needle. I want to run to my grandparents' house. They represent total protection, a refuge I love. And I want to go there. But I get the shot instead.

I always had that reflex to run away when people tried to force something on me or when I didn't understand. Whether it was finishing my soup, getting a shot, or submitting to any kind of constraint, I reacted the only way I could because I was unable to talk. Action was a substitute for discourse. In all truthfulness, I should say that my instinct to flee meshed with my personal character when it came to taking orders. I'm by nature independent, determined, and stubborn. Maybe the loneliness of silence accentuated those traits. It's "tifikul" to say.

Chapter 7

My Name Is "I"

They taught me how to say my name at school. Emmanuelle. But Emmanuelle was a little like someone detached from me, a double. When I referred to myself, I would say,

"Emmanuelle can't hear you . . ."

"Emmanuelle did this or that . . ."

I carried within me a deaf girl named Emmanuelle, and I would try to speak for her, as though we were two separate people.

I knew how to say other words. I could pronounce some of them fairly well and others, not so well. The speech therapy method involved placing my hand on the therapist's throat to feel the vibrations as the therapist vocalized. We learned the letter *r*. It vibrated like "ra." Then we learned *f* and *sh* sounds. *Sh* was a problem for me. It never came out right. We went from consonants to vowels (with more emphasis on consonants), and then on to entire words. We repeated the same word for hours. I would imitate what I saw on the therapist's lips, with my hand on her neck, copying her like a little monkey.

Each time we pronounced a word, a sound frequency would register on the screen of a machine. Little green lines, like the ones on an electrocardiogram in hospitals, danced before my eyes. You were supposed to follow the little lines that would rise and fall, level out, jump up, and dip back down.

What was a word on that screen to me? It was the amount of energy I had to put out so that my little green line would go as high as the therapist's. It was tiring and I repeated word after word without understanding what they meant. It was nothing but a throat exercise, a kind of parroting.

Deaf people can't all learn to speak and it's a lie to say otherwise. Even for those who do, their capacity for oral expression remains limited.

I was going to be seven years old at the beginning of the next school year, and I was still at the kindergarten level. But my life and the confined universe in which I was evolving, mostly in silence, were both about to change dramatically.

My father heard something on the radio. That something was a miracle in the making. I couldn't even have begun to imagine it. I considered the radio a mysterious object that talked to hearing people. I didn't pay much attention to it. But that day my father said a deaf person was talking on the program *France-Culture!* It was Alfredo Corrado, an actor and director. My father explained to my mother that he was speaking silently through sign language. It was a real language based on movements of the hands and body, and facial expressions, too! An interpreter, American like Corrado, was translating orally into French for the listeners.

Corrado said he had founded the International Visual Theater (IVT), the deaf theater in Vincennes, in 1976. He worked in the United States. There was a university in Washington, D.C., called Gallaudet University that had been created for the deaf, and he had studied there.

My father was stunned. Deaf people capable of going to college! Here in France, they could barely get through the sixth grade!

He was both ecstatic and angered.

He was angered because, as a doctor, he had trusted his colleagues. The pediatricians, ear-nose-throat specialists, speech therapists, and educators had all told him the only way to help get me out of my isolation was to have me learn spoken language. But no one had given him any information about sign language. It was the first time he had heard of it, and what's more, he heard it from a deaf person!

He was ecstatic because in Vincennes, just outside Paris, maybe there was—surely there was—a solution for me! He wanted to take me there. He was ready to give it a try because he suffered so much from not being able to talk with me.

Mother said she didn't want to go with him. She was afraid of being traumatized and maybe disappointed, too. Since she was about to give birth, she decided to let my father take me to Vincennes. She sensed that the baby she was carrying wasn't deaf. She could tell the difference between the child still nestled in her womb and me. That baby moved around and reacted to exterior noises. I, on the other hand, had slept all too quietly, sheltered from the racket. For the time being, her first concern was the arrival of the family's second child, almost seven years after me. She needed peace and quiet, time for herself. I can understand how the emotions sparked by this new ray of hope might have been too overwhelming for her. She was afraid of being disappointed again. And besides, we had our own system of communicating, what I call the "umbilical" method. We had gotten used to it. But my father had nothing. He realized I was a natural for communicating with others. It was something I was always trying to do. So he was excited by the new prospect that had miraculously come his way via the radio.

I think that when he gave me the priceless gift of sign language, it was the first time he truly accepted my deafness. It was a gift to himself too, since he wanted desperately to be able to talk to me.

Of course I didn't understand a thing and had no idea what was going on. My father looked perplexed. That's the only memory I have of that day that was so very moving for him and so incredibly fantastic for me: the radio and his face. The next day, he took me to Vincennes.

I can still see some of the visual imprints of that day: We're going up some stairs. We enter a large room. My father is talking to two hearing people—two adults who aren't wearing hearing aids. Therefore, I assume they aren't deaf. At this stage of my life, I recognize deaf people only because of their hearing aids. But, as it turns out, one is deaf and the other isn't. One is Alfredo Corrado and the other Bill Moody, a hearing sign language interpreter.

I see Alfredo and Bill signing to each other. I see that my father can understand Bill because Bill is speaking. But the signs mean nothing to me. They're quick, strange, complicated. I've never seen anything like it before. The simplistic code I invented with my mother was based on mime and a few orally pronounced words. I look at the two men in amazement. Their hands and fingers are moving, their bodies too, and they're making facial expressions. It's beautiful and mesmerizing.

Who's deaf and who's hearing? There's no way to tell. Then I realize, "Hey, that's a hearing person talking with his hands!"

Alfredo Corrado is a tall, handsome, Italian-looking man—thin with very dark hair. He has a mustache and rather sharp features. Bill has straight, medium-length hair, blue eyes, and a cheerful face. He's friendly and open. They both seem around the same age as my father.

Jean Gremion, the founder and head of the deaf social and cultural center, is there, too. He greets us.

Alfredo comes up to me and says, "I'm deaf, like you, and I sign. That's my language."

I mime my response, "Why aren't you wearing a hearing aid?"

He smiles. It's obvious that he thinks deaf people don't need hearing aids. But for me, hearing aids are a visible point of reference.

So Alfredo is deaf, but doesn't wear a hearing aid. What's more, he's an adult. I think it took me awhile to grasp that threefold oddity.

What I did realize right away, however, was that I wasn't alone in the world. It was a startling revelation. And a bewildering one because, up till then, I had thought, as do so many deaf children, that I was unique and predestined to die as a child. I discovered that I could have a future since Alfredo was a deaf adult!

That cruel logic about early death persists as long as deaf children haven't encountered a deaf adult. They need to be able to identify with an adult. It's crucial. Parents of deaf children should be made aware of the importance of having their children come in contact with deaf adults as soon as possible, right after birth. The two worlds need to blend—the world of sound and the world of silence. A deaf child's psychological development will be quicker and much better, and the child will grow up free of the pain of being alone in the world with no constructed thought patterns and no future.

Imagine that you had a kitten and never showed it a full-grown cat. It might spend its entire life thinking it was a kitten. Or imagine that the little cat only lived with dogs. It would think it was the only cat in the world and wear itself out trying to communicate in dog language. The cat might succeed at getting a few basic things across to the dogs through motions— eating, drinking, fear, affection, submission or aggressiveness. But it would be so much happier and more well-balanced among its own kind, young and old, speaking cat!

With the oral technique that had been imposed on my parents from the beginning, I had no chance of meeting deaf adults who could serve as role models for me because my parents had been advised against it. I only had contact with hearing people.

I don't have a precise recollection of that first, stupefying visit to Vincennes when I watched in awe as all those hands whirled about. I don't know what my father and the two men said to each other. I just remember my astonishment at seeing my father understand what Alfredo's hands and Bill's mouth were saying. At the time, I still didn't know that because of those men I was going to acquire a language. What stuck in my mind, though, was the stupendous revelation that Emmanuelle would be able to grow up! That was something I had seen now with my very own eyes.

The following week, my father took me back to Vincennes. They were having a parent-child communication workshop. There were lots of parents. Alfredo had the children gather in a circle around him and began working with them. He demonstrated some signs. The parents watched so they could learn, too. They were simple signs, I remember, like "house," "eat," "drink," "sleep," "table."

He drew a house on a flipboard and showed us the corresponding sign. Then he drew a picture of an adult and said, "This is your daddy. You are your daddy's daughter. This is your mommy. You are your mommy's daughter."

He also showed us someone looking for something, first through mime, next using sign. Then he asked, "Where's Mommy?"

I signed, "Mommy is somewhere else."

Then he corrected me.

"Where's Mommy? Mommy is at home. Make the sign for 'Mommy' and 'house.'"

A complete sentence: "Mommy is at home." Finally at the age of seven, I was signing with both hands to identify my mother and designate where she was!

Elated, with my eyes fixed on Alfredo's, I used both hands to repeat, "Mommy is at home."

The first few times I was there, I learned everyday words and then people's names. He was Alfredo, I was Emmanuelle. A sign for him and a sign for me.

Emmanuelle: "Sun-Coming-from-the-Heart." "Emmanuelle" was my name to hearing people, "Sun-Coming-from-the-Heart" was my name to deaf people.

That was the first time I realized you could give people names. That, too, was fantastic. Except for Mommy and Daddy, I didn't know that people in our family had names. I used to meet people, friends of my parents or members of the family, but, in my mind, they didn't have names. There was no way to define them. I was so surprised to learn that his name was Alfredo and the other man was Bill. And me, especially me, Emmanuelle. I finally understood that I had an identity. I, Emmanuelle.

Until then, when I talked about myself, it was like talking about somebody else. Somebody who wasn't "I." People would always say, "Emmanuelle is deaf." It was always "She can't hear you, she can't hear you." There was no "I." I was "she."

People who have had their name in their head practically from birth, a name that Mommy and Daddy repeated, might find that hard to understand. They're used to turning their head when their name is called. Their identity is given to them at birth. They don't have to think about it or ask themselves questions about who they are. They're "I" or "me." It's natural and effortless. They know who they are. They can identify themselves, introduce themselves to people with a symbol that stands for them. But the deaf Emmanuelle didn't know that she was "I," that she was "me." She discovered it with sign language, and now she knew. Emmanuelle could say, "My name is Emmanuelle."

It was a joy to make that discovery. Emmanuelle was no longer that double whose needs, desires, dislikes, and woes I had to painfully explain. I had discovered the world around me and myself in the midst of it.

It was also at that time, when I started seeing deaf adults on a regular basis, that I stopped being afraid of dying. I never thought about it again. And I had my father to thank for that.

It was like being born again. My life was just beginning. The first barrier had fallen. There were still others around me, but an initial opening had been made in my prison wall. I was going to understand the world with my eyes and hands. I could already sense it and I was so eager!

There before me stood the marvelous man who was teaching me about the world, and the names of people and things. There was a sign for Bill, one for Alfredo, one for Jacques (my father), one for my mother, my sister, the house, the table, the cat . . . I was going to live! And I had so many questions to ask. So many! I was voracious, starved for answers because now people could answer me!

In the beginning, I mixed up all the different communication methods: signs and mime and words that came out orally. I was a bit unsettled, confused. Sign language had happened so suddenly. I was seven years old and had to get things straight in my mind, sort out all the information I was taking in. And there was a good deal of it. You really become a communicating individual, capable of developing, when, for example, you're finally able to use correctly constructed language to say things like, "My name is Emmanuelle. I'm hungry. Mommy is at home, Daddy is with me. My friend's name is Jules, my cat's name is Bobbin."

I didn't learn everything all at once, of course. At home, I continued using a little of the code my mother and I had made up, but started mixing in some sign. I remember they understood me, but I don't recall my first complete signed sentence that they comprehended.

Little by little, I straightened things out in my head and began to construct ideas and organize thoughts. Most importantly, I started communicating with my father.

Then my mother joined us in Vincennes. She, too, was about to emerge from the tunnel of erroneous information and false hopes my parents had been trapped in ever since I was born. She was totally surprised to see that there was a meeting place for the deaf. It was a vibrant, creative place, where they were being taught. It was a place to get to know parents trying to cope with the same problems, to meet professionals specializing in deafness who were rethinking the practices of the medical profession and the information it was disseminating. They had made the decision to teach a language. Sign language. Not a code or jargon, but a real language.

"I was terribly frightened," says my mother in recalling her first visit to Vincennes. "I was face to face with reality. It was like a second diagnosis. Everyone was friendly, but as I listened to the deaf people tell of their suffering as children, of the horrible isolation they had lived in before, of their problems as adults and their ongoing struggle, I was sick. I had been wrong. I had been misled by people who had told me, 'With speech therapy and a hearing aid, she'll be able to speak.'"

"After you were born," my father says, "I could practically hear them say, or at least I wanted to hear them say, 'One day, she WILL HEAR.'"

Vincennes was another world, the real deaf world, devoid of needless patronizing. But it was also a world of hope for the deaf. Sure, deaf people manage to talk, more or less, yet for many of us who are profoundly deaf, it's never more than partially effective. Now, with sign language, plus speech, and my all-consuming desire to communicate, I was going to make tremendous strides.

After seven years of existence, I had just taken a huge step forward. My name is "I."

Chapter 8

Marie, Marie

When my little sister was born, I asked what her name was. Marie.

Marie, Marie. I had trouble remembering it. I decided to write it down on paper, over and over, like practicing words at school. I kept going back to my mother to ask her what my little sister's name was. I wanted to be sure. And I would repeat it: "Ma-rie, Ma-rie, Ma-rie . . ."

I'm Emmanuelle. She's Marie.

Marie, Marie, Marie . . .

"What's her name again?"

I wrote it more than a hundred times, letter by letter, to be able to remember it visually. But it was still too hard to pronounce. I had to really work at saying her name.

My father took me to the hospital to see my little sister. I hated hospitals. When Mother was pregnant, I saw her having blood samples taken. I was so afraid, I hid under the bed. Even today, I can't stand the sight of blood. I loathe needles. *Hospital* means needles and blood. *Hospital* means threatening place.

My sister was in an incubator. She wasn't premature, but since the hospital wasn't heated, they put her in there with a few other babies to keep warm.

I don't know if I was happy when I saw her. What I saw mystified me—the incubator and a tiny little thing inside. It was hard to imagine anything about her, there behind the plastic. I can't really remember, but my feelings at that moment weren't very clear. I wondered to myself, "Are both of us the same?"

I don't know if I actually asked that question, but when I saw the baby, my reaction was mostly one of surprise. I had a vague feeling of apprehension. Was she going to grow up?

Mother came home from the hospital and her stomach wasn't big any more. It was flat. I don't think I understood how the baby had come out. There was a baby. But how had it come out? The link between the baby they showed me and my mother's flat stomach was not at all obvious to me. Maybe the baby had come out of her mouth or ears. It was confusing and very mysterious.

Naturally, everyone in the family wanted to know if Marie was deaf. My mother had already set her mind at ease during her pregnancy because she noticed that Marie moved a lot. When she slammed a door shut, she could feel the baby react. It kicked inside her. I could see that Marie was different from me. But Mother asked a specialist to confirm it. Her instinct wasn't enough. She wanted to be told.

My little sister was hearing. I had a little sister who was hearing, "like the others." I understood that she was like my parents and that it was three against one.

I imagine that in the beginning I thought, "Maybe she'll be like me, and together we'll be stronger." I felt a little like an outsider in my family at that age. I didn't have a bond with anyone like myself. I wasn't able to identify with them. But I don't think the difference between her and me upset me.

When Mother came home from the hospital with her, I was happy to see the tiny baby in her arms. They put her in my arms and gave me all sorts of pointers. They told me to hold her head because she was delicate. I was afraid to break her, and carried her very carefully.

I noticed that the little "thing" was alive. You had to be careful and not jolt her around like a doll. I was a little scared.

Before she arrived, my parents spoiled me a lot. They showered all their attention on me. Now their attention was for her and so I knew things had changed.

Every time Marie cried, my mother would go running to her crib. She heard her and knew when she was hungry or wanted to sleep. I was bothered by that.

I told my mother I didn't want to have children when I grew up. At first, she didn't understand why I felt that way. What was going on in my head? Was I jealous of my sister because she wasn't like me?

No. The reason I decided at seven not to have children was simpler and more significant. With some degree of difficulty, I finally made my mother understand that my fear stemmed from the fact that I wouldn't be able to hear my child cry. Therefore, I wouldn't be able to go running, like my mother, to console my baby and help it when it needed me. I saw that as an insurmountable problem. Consequently, I wouldn't have children.

"A mother senses when her child is crying," my mother said. "She has a special relationship with her child. You don't necessarily have to hear."

Being able to sense was not enough of an answer for me. I wanted to able to hear my child. I was too afraid.

Since I couldn't see any way of dealing with the situation except by not having children, my mother suggested I talk about it with some of the deaf adults at Vincennes, "They're in a better position than your father or me to answer you."

The answer they gave me at Vincennes was so simple it surprised me: You just put a special microphone under the baby's pillow that makes a light flash when the baby cries.

It all became clear to me. One day I'd be a mother. I could be a mother, too.

There were thousands of questions like that running through my head at the time. I would love to be able draw up a list if I could just remember them all. But I can't.

My relationship with the outside world at that age was very peculiar. I often found myself alone and bored in the midst of a world of talkers. Sometimes I got aggravated when I couldn't understand. Except for my parents, it seemed that people weren't trying very hard to talk to me. My world was limited to my parents and Marie, who still couldn't talk, but who babbled and cried and laughed, and who was the center of attention. Sometimes I would say, "I'm here too!"

And they'd answer me, "But you're not the only one now. There's somebody else. You have to learn to share."

It's not easy in the beginning to share your parents' affection. I wanted to be pampered just as much as before.

I felt comfortable with other deaf children. I wanted to teach them my new language at school but we were in an oral class and sign language wasn't allowed. So I had to practice signing during recess. I tried to explain to my classmates that you didn't say Daddy and Mommy like in speech therapy, but with signs. They didn't seem to care and wondered what crazy things I was telling them. They were the same age as me, but whether they said Daddy in code or in sign made no difference to them. I recognized the difference though. I couldn't quite put my finger on it, but I knew I wasn't the same as before. A small revolution had taken place inside me and I wanted to share it with them. I wanted to take those deaf children and shake them up, to open the world for them the way it had been opened for me. I wanted them to be able to express themselves freely, to be able to make "flowers in space" with their hands, as Alfredo Corrado would say.

I was starting to sign well. Between my courses at the IVT and my mainstream classes, I was making real headway. More so at the IVT than at school where they were still teaching me that three little cars plus one little car make four, having me write A's and B's endlessly, having me read lips, and wearing me out by having me repeat the same syllable over and over with the speech therapist. I think hearing parents who deprive their children of sign language will never understand what goes on in the mind of a deaf child. There's loneliness, resistance, a craving to communicate, and sometimes anger. At home, you feel excluded by your family when everyone is talking and not paying any attention to you. Because you always have to ask, always tug at someone's sleeve or skirt to know just a little, a tiny little bit, of what's going on around you. Otherwise, life is like a silent film without captions.

I'm lucky to have the parents I do—a father who made a beeline for Vincennes to learn sign language and a mother who followed the same path and didn't rap me on the fingers out of ignorance when I signed, "I love you, Mommy."

The parents of most of the children in my class supported the oral method. Their children would never take sign language courses at Vincennes. They would spend years trying to make their throats into sound boxes and to form words whose meaning they didn't always understand.

I didn't care for the teachers in that so-called mainstream class. They wanted to make me like the hearing children. They forced me to talk and wouldn't let me sign. They made us feel we had to hide the fact that we were deaf. We couldn't get half of what they were saying in class. Even so, we had to imitate them like little robots. But at the IVT, I was with both deaf children and deaf adults, and I felt more at ease.

That year held some lighter moments for my family—like when I lost my first baby tooth. The day it happened, my grandparents told me the story about the little mouse that puts a coin under children's pillows. I imagined that the mouse was like the ones in cartoons, with cute little pointed ears. It wasn't just a story. It was a fact. And I was going to make sure it was true.

That night, I dutifully put my precious tooth under my pillow and went to sleep hoping the little mouse would show up. I wasn't at all frightened at the thought of the mouse crawling into my bed. When I woke up the next morning, I found a five franc coin, along with a drawing of a mouse. The mouse had really come to see me! I was all excited and, since I had kept my tooth, I decided to do it again the following night. I think the idea I had in mind was to check and see if the little mouse was really a little mouse.

Sure enough, the next day, I found another coin, but the tooth was gone! I ran to ask my grandparents what had happened to it. They explained that the little mouse had taken it.

I was furious. First of all because it was MY tooth, and secondly because I wanted to try it again. I was really furious. It was MY tooth!

There's another image I'll never forget. One night, we were getting ready to go visit some friends of my parents. I was wearing a beautiful dress and everything was perfect. My mother got the baby all set and then gave her to me to hold while she gathered her things. All of a sudden, the baby had a strange look on her face and I could tell she had messed her diaper. There I was in my pretty dress holding a baby who had gone all over me! I got upset. I had to put on another dress and Marie had to have her diaper changed! I wasn't at all pleased.

I don't know why, but I'll never forget that scene. It may have been my first encounter with another individual's reality. I had to take somebody else's life into account within the family bubble that had previously been reserved for me.

When Marie was just a toddler, I would say "the baby" because I couldn't remember how to pronounce her name correctly. I often wanted to say "Marie, look at me," so I could speak to her in sign language, but I couldn't. She was too little and I wasn't very proficient yet myself. So I tried to talk to her the way my parents did, voicing a little, using my own awkwardly pronounced words.

"Ma-rie . . . Ma-rie . . . Ma-rie . . ."

Chapter 9

City of the Deaf

I was just beginning to learn sign language when we left for Washington, D.C., the fantastic "city of the deaf."

My parents decided to leave Marie behind in France. Now that I look back, I'm rather embarrassed about that. They should have brought her along. I deprived her of our parents for a whole month. They decided to entrust her to our grandparents. I wasn't to blame for the situation, but it bothers me a little. They really went out of their way for me by leaving the baby and going there to learn sign language.

Going to Washington meant taking a plane. I had never flown before, and didn't know where I was headed. I knew it was on the other side of the ocean. But where? Who could explain Washington, D.C., to me? Actually, no one could when we were getting ready to go, but later, once we were there, it all became crystal clear.

The trip was arranged by Bernard Mottez, a French sociologist, and Harry Markowicz, an American linguist. With us were Bill Moody, Alfredo Corrado's interpreter with the IVT, Dominique Hof, a speech therapist, and deaf adults working with deaf children. The purpose of the trip was to learn how deaf Americans lived, to get to know their university, Gallaudet, and to see how they coped on a daily basis.

Claire was the only child my age in the group. She was a little blond girl, deaf like me, who became my closest friend. She was as lively as I was shy and reserved. I'll never forget the first time I saw her face. When our eyes met, the attraction was instantaneous. We were setting off together on an extraordinary adventure, both of us still unaware of the joys of discovery it held.

The take-off frightened me. The ground rumbled as the wheels jolted along. I felt the plane shake and then a kind of air pocket, like an elevator going too fast. I felt crushed against the back of my seat.

Once we were in the air, I was okay. Claire and I sat quietly reading a Mickey Mouse book; then we slept until the plane began to land. That's when my ears started to hurt so much I wanted to bite the seat cushion. It was really painful and took me by complete surprise. I felt like I was going to explode. They told me to chew gum. I chewed and chewed, but the pain didn't subside. Claire didn't feel a thing, so she was wild with excitement.

Once we were on the ground, I started to feel better and the pain slowly went away. We were in New York. I can't remember much about it except for the skyscrapers.

Then we left for Washington, by bus this time. It was sunny and humid. We arrived at what seemed like a huge residence hall where my parents and Claire's had rooms.

Outside, I was amazed at what I saw. It was more than surprising; it was revolutionary! And then it hit me: I was in a city of deaf people. They were signing everywhere—on the sidewalks, in the stores, all over the Gallaudet University campus. Deaf people were all over the place. A store owner was signing to a customer, people were saying hello to each other and conversing in sign. I was really in a deaf city. I imagined that everyone in Washington was deaf. It was like landing on another planet where everyone was like me.

"Mommy, Daddy, look! Deaf people talking!"

There were two, three, four of them talking together, then five, six . . . I couldn't believe my eyes! I stared at them with my mouth wide open in disbelief. I was bowled over. It was mind-boggling. Groups of deaf people engaged in real conversation. That was something I had never seen before.

I tried to understand where I was and what was happening, but couldn't. Actually, there wasn't anything to understand except that I had been catapulted into a deaf world at the age of seven.

We took our first stroll around the Gallaudet campus. Alfredo Corrado explained that not everyone was deaf. It only seemed that way because, although many of the professors were hearing, they knew sign language. They weren't wearing labels on their foreheads. How could I recognize them? It didn't really seem to matter. They all looked so happy and relaxed. There wasn't the same reluctance I detected elsewhere, even at the school in Vincennes. In France, people were unconsciously embarrassed about using sign language, and I sensed that embarrassment. They would rather hide, as if it were something to be ashamed of. I know of deaf people who were tormented throughout their childhood by feelings of humiliation, and who even to this day haven't fully adjusted to their language. You can tell things haven't been easy for them, perhaps because sign language was prohibited in France until 1976. It was considered an indecent, provocative, sensual form of communication because it involved using the body.

But there was none of that feeling in Washington. No problems. Everyone was so wonderfully at ease. The people there used sign language in a natural way without being self-conscious about it. No one hid or felt ashamed. In fact, deaf people there had a certain pride. They had their culture and their language, like anyone else.

Bill Moody took us around the city and translated in French, English, ASL (American Sign Language), and LSF (Langue des Signes Française/French Sign Language) all at the same time. It was a fascinating display of gymnastics. I never figured out how he did it. Every country has its own sign language, as it does its own culture. But two deaf foreigners usually manage to understand each other fairly quickly. We have a sort of basic international code that allows us to catch on relatively easily. For example, people obviously eat with their mouths, not with their ears. So when you have a sign that involves opening your mouth and pointing to it with your finger, it's pretty clear what that means. The same is true for *house.* I didn't understand the first time someone said *home* to me in English. But as soon as they made the sign for "house," in the shape of a roof, I got it. As for abstract concepts and nuances, every sign language requires some getting used to, just like any foreign language.

We stayed in Washington for a month, in a dorm at Gallaudet University. Everyone in the building could sign. We had our meals in the cafeteria and had to give our meal ticket number in sign language to be served.

I was proud, prouder than I had ever been before. There were deaf doctors, deaf lawyers, and deaf psychology professors at the university. All of them had completed programs of higher learning. I looked upon them as geniuses, gods! There was nothing like it in France.

I remember an impressive and touching encounter with a deaf-blind woman. I wondered how people communicated with her.

They told me to fingerspell my name in the palm of her hand. She smiled at me and repeated my name in my hand. I was deeply moved by that woman. She was terrific. I thought all blind people kept their eyes shut. But she had a look that looked right at me, as though she could really see me. I asked her what she did to talk since she couldn't spell every word in people's hands.

She explained in sign, "You talk to me in sign language. I cup my hands around yours to feel each sign, and I can understand you."

It was all too puzzling. I needed my eyes to understand sign language. I had to be facing the person. Did she understand? Really? I asked my question again.

"Don't worry, I understand you. There's no problem."

I wondered how she had grown up, how she had been able to learn. I was terribly impressed by her hands softly enveloping mine and following the shape of each sign in space. It was even harder for her than for me. Her predicament was worse than mine yet she was able to communicate!

The hope that those people in Washington gave me, their positive outlook, led me to yet another discovery, a very important one about myself: I finally understood I was deaf. No one had told me that yet.

One night in Washington, I came bursting into my parents' room, all excited. A real bundle of energy. They couldn't understand me because I was signing so fast. I began again, this time more slowly, "I'm deaf!"

"I'm deaf" didn't mean "I can't hear." It meant "I *realize* I'm deaf."

It was a positive, decisive statement. I was admitting in my mind the fact that I was deaf. I understood it and analyzed it because I had been given a language that allowed me to do that. I understood that my parents had their language, their way of communicating, and that I had mine. I belonged to a community and had a true identity. I had compatriots.

In Washington, they told me, "You're like us, you're deaf." And they showed me the sign for deaf. No one had ever SAID that to me. That was a revelation, because I hadn't constructed the concept in my mind yet. I was still at the stage where I defined myself in terms like "Emmanuelle doesn't hear you."

Earlier, I had understood the concept of "I." "I'm called Emmanuelle." That evening, like a flash of lighting, I understood: "I'm deaf."

Now I knew what I was going to do. I would be like them, since I was deaf like them. I would learn, work, live, and talk, because they did. I was going to find happiness because they had.

I saw happy deaf people all around me. People with a future. Adults. They had occupations, and someday I would have one, too. I had suddenly been made aware of my strong points, my capabilities, my potential. Now I had hope.

That day, I grew up mentally. A lot. I had become a human being endowed with language. Hearing people, like my parents, used their voices. I used my hands. It was just a different language. The same as Claire's. Plenty of people used it.

After that, the questions began to flow. First of all, how do you communicate with hearing people? There was no problem with my parents. I was lucky that they had accepted my language and taken the trouble to learn it. But what about other people?

The answer was obvious. I had to continue learning to speak orally. I had to do my bit, too, and accept hearing people the way my parents had accepted me. They could sign. I was going to speak with my voice, the way you learn a foreign language.

Bill Moody was terrific with us. He helped my parents discover the deaf world. He was patient, always clear, and always there for us. His expressive blue eyes and nimble, precise hands made him a remarkable teacher and guide.

I spent every waking moment learning to sign. I saw signs everywhere and would practice them in front of a mirror. My head was full of them. Sometimes I had to close my eyes to remember, to blot out everything else till the sign came back. Once in a while, I couldn't understand my signing when I looked at myself. I wanted to say something, but it came out too fast and looked like gobbledygook. I would even invent signs because I didn't know them all yet and I was adamant about saying what I wanted to say. When no one understood, I would explain the sign—"For me that means this."

"We don't say it like that. We say this!"

"Oh! Really?"

I picked up signs with astonishing speed, faster than my parents. It was harder for them. What would take them two years took me three months.

When I discovered sign language, it was like finding the giant key that opened the giant door separating me from the world. I could understand both the deaf and hearing worlds. I came to realize that the world didn't stop with my parents. There were other interesting people, too. I had outgrown my early innocence. I looked at situations head on. My thought processes were becoming more structured. I felt the need to talk. I wanted to say everything, tell everything, and understand everything.

It was wild. I was becoming a real chatterbox. I think I must have annoyed everybody with all my questions. "What did you say?"

When we got back to Paris, Marie was totally confused. Before we left, everyone spoke to her orally, but now we were all using sign language! It was after that trip that I resolved to teach her how to sign as soon as I could. I was already impatiently eying her little hands, eager to see her talk to me. Eager to be her teacher. I was anxious for her to grow up so I could talk with her.

Marie was to become more than my sister, special confidant, and interpreter. Little by little, the unique relationship I had with my mother was transferred to her.

But for the time being, I had to work hard to talk to her. I had to accept the fact that I wasn't alone any more and learn to share.

We used to take baths together. I would annoy her by grabbing one of her toys. She'd splash water, then so would I. She'd pull my hair and I'd pull hers. We enjoyed getting each other mad. I loved seeing her little teeth sparkle when she cried so Mother would come running. It made me laugh. My mother would rush in angrily and scold me. Then I'd cry and it was Marie's turn to roar with laughter.

To make the sign for "Marie," you join your hands together over your chest.

I adore Marie.

Chapter 10
Crying Flower

I don't know how old I was when I started to understand the difference between fiction and reality. But because my points of reference are essentially visual, I think movies must have had something to do with it. When I was little, I saw the black and white version of *Tarzan* starring Johnny Weissmuller. It seemed completely real and believable to me. Tarzan couldn't talk, so in my mind it was real. That visual image left its mark on me. I equated him with a deaf person who couldn't talk. I imagined he was like me, unable to communicate. After seeing the film, I had bad dreams. The scene where a tribe of black savages comes in yelling, and shrieks and dances around Tarzan really gave me a scare. I couldn't figure out what was going on and I had nightmares about it. My parents tried to explain the plot to me, but I couldn't understand it. Later, I found out that poor Tarzan had lost his parents, and the tribe of black "bad guys" was furious. But it was too late. I had already been having nightmares, most likely because I identified with Tarzan's muteness. That was before I learned sign language, so there was still a lot of confusion in my mind.

Then I began discovering the meaning of words. I've forgotten how I came to know what they meant. A hearing child can associate written words with the sounds he or she hears, and then with their meaning.

I must have written the word "Mommy" twenty times. But did I really understand what it meant at the time? Did it refer to my own mother who was standing in front of me? Or to someone else? Did it correspond to "table"? I've forgotten how I learned sentences, meanings, and structures.

I loved it when they used to tell me stories. Then I learned to read . . . and did I ever! I always had my nose in a dictionary, looking things up and memorizing them. At first, I used to read *Asterix and Obelix* comic books without understanding the words. I followed the story by looking at the pictures. It was a silent process.

In real life, I always sensed that I wasn't in sync with the scenes that unfolded before my eyes. I always had the impression I wasn't in the same film as the people around me. Sometimes that made me react in unexpected ways.

FLASHBACK:

There's a party at our house. Everyone's talking. There are only hearing people there. I feel isolated as usual in situations like that. I'm perplexed by the mystery of how communication is possible between those people. How do they manage to all speak at once with their backs turned and their bodies facing any which way? What do their voices sound like? I've never heard my mother's or father's voice, or the voices of my friends. The mouths of all those people at the party are moving, opening and closing really fast. Their lips smile. I observe intently and then get tired. Boredom, intense boredom, takes hold of me. I'm back in a desert of exclusion. Suddenly, Maurice Fanon, a singer and friend my uncle invited to the party, comes up to me and hands me a flower. I take the flower and burst into tears. Everybody's looking at me. My mother asks what's going on.

What was going on, really? I don't know. I was experiencing a powerful emotion. And was it too strong for me in my state of isolation? Was crying the only way I could express it? Was the gap between them and me that big? Were the situations and things people were doing that incomprehensible? Possibly.

I still wonder why I broke down and cried so much over that flower. I'd love to know, but I just can't explain it.

From birth to age seven, I had lots of nightmares, that's for sure. Everything I didn't understand during the day must have been knocking around in my head. Idea associations were all bouncing helter-skelter.

Praise be to my father who opened the world to me by taking me to Vincennes and Washington, D.C., and who told me, "Come on, we're going to learn sign language together!"

After our trip to Washington, I started to worry about what would become of me later. What kind of job would I have? How would I live? With whom? I had grown up so much mentally, had latched onto so many things, and there was still so much more.

When we got back from the United States, my father decided that he would provide psychiatric treatment for the deaf. At *Sainte-Anne* Hospital, in Paris, he started the first out-patient practice where sign language was used, and later broadened the service to include in-hospital care. Yes, deaf people can have psychological problems like anyone else.

As a child, the image I had of my father was one of an intellectual. He's a psychiatrist and, in the beginning, I used to tell everyone, "My father works with crazy people!"

Since my mother teaches children with psychological problems, I used to say the same thing about her, "Mommy teaches crazy people."

I had trouble grasping what those two occupations were all about. Little by little, I began to understand. My father would say, "I'm a psychiatrist and psychoanalyst. I meet with people and psychoanalyze them."

"Psychoanalyst. Isn't that like a psychiatrist?"

"No. A psychiatrist's job is different. You have to have a medical degree to be a psychiatrist and prescribe medication. Understand? I prescribe treatments for people. But I do psychoanalysis, too!"

I really wanted to know what that word *psychoanalysis* meant. It mystified and confused me. We often talked about all those *psych* words with my father.

One day he explained Freud to me. He told me about the discovery of the concepts of psychoanalysis regarding the child, pleasure, joy, the oral and anal stages, etc. I was eleven. It was "tifikul."

I finally got it, but for a long time, I used the sign "crazy people doctor" when talking to my deaf friends about my father's work. Sorry, Dad.

I also fused the first letter of his name, "*J*" with the sign you make next to your head to mean "on the moon." My father is often absent-minded, so he's "Jacques-on-the-Moon."

Deaf people give special name signs to everyone. The deaf people at Vincennes decided to name my mother "Rabbit-Teeth" because of her slightly protruding teeth.

"No way. I refuse to be called Rabbit-Teeth," said my mother.

So we gave her another name that suits her very well: "Anne-the-Fighter." The *A* is signed with the arm raised forward, thumb out, and fist clenched. It made her laugh. She could almost see herself singing the battle cry from the refrain of the Internationale.

Other people were given name signs like "Big-Hair" and "Big-Nose." My good friend, Bill Moody, Alfredo's interpreter in Washington, has the name sign "Thumb-under-the-Nose" because he's constantly wiping an ever-present drop of moisture off the tip of his nose with his thumb!

In sign language, we focus on a visual characteristic that is indicative of a behavioral trait, a tic, or a physical feature. It's much easier than always fingerspelling a person's name. Sometimes it's funny, sometimes poetic, but it's always accurate. Hearing people don't like it very much. Some are offended, but not deaf people.

To make the sign for French President Mitterrand, you put your hand in front of your mouth with the little and index fingers extended to suggest two canine teeth, like vampire fangs. Everybody knows that, before he had his teeth filed down, Mitterrand had two splendid canines. Politician Raymond Barr is "Fat-Cheeks." Actor Gerard Depardieu's sign is a big nose with two bumps. Jacques Chirac's sign is a pointed nose in the form of a *V* for victory. Those are a few examples of dominant physical features. But I have a friend whose name is "Exaggerate" because he always exaggerates whenever he tells you something. Name signs are comparable to the names Indians gave each other, like "Great Horned Beak," "Eagle Eye," or "Dances with Wolves."

Deaf people are generally cheerful. Maybe that's because they suffered so much as children. They derive such pleasure from exchanging ideas that cheerfulness prevails. When you have a group of deaf people talking, whether on a playground or in a restaurant, it's incredibly lively. They talk and talk, sometimes for hours on end. It's as though they had a tremendous yearning to tell each other things, from the most superficial to the most serious.

The deaf might have named me "Crying-Flower" if I hadn't been given access to their linguistic community. But at seven, I became chatty and radiant. Sign language was my light, my sun. I never stopped. Things just kept coming out, like through a great opening to the light. I couldn't stop talking to people. I became "Sun-Coming-from-the-Heart."

It's a beautiful sign.

Chapter 11
Forbidden to Forbid

I often asked deaf adults questions I had already asked my parents because I always felt that the answers they had been giving me were incomplete or unsatisfactory. And sometimes I didn't get any answers at all. But my relationship with my mother was still very strong, especially when it came to education and learning words. If I had to define it, I would say it was pedagogical and structured. Things were more relaxed with my father. We played games, listened to music, and joked around. In all other aspects, though, he was an intellectual. He's an avid reader. When I was little, I could tell he wasn't really coming down to my level. Now that I'm an adult, I understand him perfectly. Everything has changed in our relationship.

Thanks to my parents, I wasn't behind in school. I had made great progress.

When I was eleven, they wanted to put me in the French equivalent of middle school at the *Collège Molière,* but their request was denied. Denied, even though I had passed the entrance exam!

"Your daughter is profoundly deaf. It's out of the question."

My parents were furious with the public school system, and I was completely discouraged. How was I going to be able to continue my schooling?

The decision to refuse me entry was a grave injustice. I took it as an act of racism. To deny a child an education because he or she is too black, too yellow, or too deaf, smacks of the worst form of segregation in a country that calls itself democratic.

In all of Paris there was only one private program specializing in deaf education that would take me: the Morvan program. I passed the entrance exam and was admitted. Both me and my profound deafness.

"You need to know, Emmanuelle," my mother warned me, "they use the oral method to teach classes at that school. There's no support in sign language. You'll have to read lips in class and you'll have to speak. You won't be allowed to use your hands. Do you understand?"

At the time, I thought I had understood what she meant, but actually I hadn't paid much attention. The word *forbidden,* if it even came up, didn't really phase me. I had passed my exam. I was eleven years old, and there were other things that interested and preoccupied me.

What interested me first and foremost was teaching Marie how to sign. She had just turned three. I was teaching her how to write a few words—simple everyday things—and showing her how to say them in sign language.

We had already developed a strong emotional bond. I thought she was just adorable and liked playing with her. I enjoyed teaching her and was proud of it.

"Look! You see? I can teach her things," I told my mother.

I let Marie have my room and slept in the living room. I had an old school desk with a wooden bench and a hole where the inkwell went. That's where I would lecture.

Marie would sit next to me on the straight bench, and we would draw. Since my mother had no luck teaching her the days of the week, I thought I'd give it a shot. We repeated the days in combination with colors: Monday was yellow, Tuesday red, etc. First, I taught her how to write, then how to sign. Her tiny hands made such pretty things in space. She caught on so quickly, I was lost in admiration. She could be speaking French and suddenly switch to sign with surprising ease. She gave me great joy and I was immensely proud of her.

I had become a source of knowledge. Now we could swap languages. It didn't matter that I was deaf and she was hearing. She understood me. There was no difference between us since I was able to teach her things and she comprehended them. She was bilingual.

Nonetheless, there was a difference. I used to watch her copy my mother when she pronounced "a, e, i, o, u." She could imitate my parents' voices. I couldn't. When I tried imitating my mother's voice, it was completely off. They would say, "Speak, speak. We understand you." But I knew very well that, in reality, that was only true for my family. At grade school, the hearing kids couldn't have cared less about me and used to laugh at me when I tried to speak. "We don't understand you! What are you saying?"

Of course they didn't understand me. But I was the one going out of my way to talk like them, without ever hearing myself. I didn't know what my voice sounded like. And how were those kids trying to reach out to me, aside from laughing at me?

I'm often asked if I miss hearing my mother's voice. You can't miss what you don't know. I don't know what the sound of birds singing is like, or the sound of waves. Or, as they tried to convey to parents of deaf children at Vincennes, the sound of an egg frying!

What does an egg frying sound like? I can imagine it in my own way. Sizzling is something that ripples. It's hot. It's hot, yellow, and white rippling.

I don't miss it. My eyes do the work. Even as a child, my imagination was surely richer than other people's. It was just a tad disorganized.

Things started getting organized in my head around the time I began middle school. That's why I fiercely rejected being labeled *handicapped* even then. I'm not handicapped, I'm deaf. I have a language I can use to express myself, and friends and parents who speak it.

FLASHBACK:
My first day in the Morvan program; I arrive late. The principal escorts me to the classroom and has me take a seat. There's a slight interruption. All eyes are on me. Then the class resumes.

I feel surrounded, as though I'm being spied on from all sides. I'm in a deaf class, and deaf people are naturally curious.

The teacher is a woman. She's careful to keep her hands behind her back and over-enunciate, dragging out her very proper mouth movements. The students are reading her lips.

At that instant, I understood the extent of the disastrous situation I was in and remembered my parents' mindful warning. The woman didn't use her hands or body to teach. Her whole posture conveyed the attitude that using anything other than spoken language was forbidden. She struck me as provoking. I was extremely shocked and completely disgusted. At the IVT in Vincennes, I had become accustomed to my language and felt comfortable with it. Here, I was an outsider again. At one point I said to myself, "This is a farce. It's got to be a joke. She'll stop in a minute. She'll straighten out."

But the students were all looking on so attentively I didn't dare interrupt. I struggled to understand what she was saying. I wasn't getting a single word and she could tell. I didn't even have any idea what subject she was teaching.

At recess time, I got to know some of my classmates. Maybe "got to know" is putting it too strongly. Not one of them knew sign language. Some spoke with their hands in a kind of code they hoped would convey what they wanted to say, but they didn't know any grammatical rules. Nevertheless, I gave it a try and signed, "What's your name? My name is Emmanuelle. I speak in sign language. Do you understand?"

No response. Wide-eyed, the kid I was talking to looked at my hands as though I were speaking Chinese. He and the others hadn't learned the grammar, inversions, referents, the entire structure of my language, like hand shapes, hand orientation, position, movement, and facial expressions. With that structure, that grammar, I can make thousands of signs, ranging from the simplest to the most subtle. Sometimes it's just a matter of changing the parameters slightly, such as direction and/or placement, etc. The possibilities are endless.

The kid's rounded eyes staring at me betrayed his total bewilderment. Another boy got the message across to me that he wanted to know my name, so I fingerspelled it for him. His eyes got bigger than the first kid's! These boys didn't even know how to use fingerspelling, the alphabet invented by the Abbé de l'Épée that you write in the air with your hand.

On my second day at school, I decided to confront the situation. I started distributing copies of the manual alphabet to explain the language of the deaf to my classmates. Scandal! Provocation! I was immediately summoned by the school administrators who proceeded to put me in my place. Gently but firmly. They told me that conducting myself like an activist, a union boss, or, at the very least, a rabble-rouser would not be tolerated.

"It is strictly forbidden to promote sign language within the walls of this institution."

"I only wanted to show them fingerspelling."

"Don't argue. Forbidden means forbidden."

And "forbidden" makes no allowances for dialog. No student at that school had the right to be informed. That was the law.

And indeed, it was the law in France. The ban remained in effect until 1991. But it was 1984 and I was eleven years old. I couldn't see into the future, and, in the meantime, I had to be subjected to the law of silence. That did it! How could the language that had made me receptive to the world and to understanding others, the language of my feelings and of everyday events be forbidden to the other kids? It was a nightmare!

A few of the teachers knew LSF (French Sign Language) and would use it in secret. Some of them even quietly came to my defense. The injustice of the situation cut me to the quick. Educators, teachers, and professors who have strong feelings about the issue should be able to express themselves openly as responsible adults. They are instrumental in shaping the lives of deaf children and assuring their psychological, emotional, and behavioral stability.

The State shouldn't turn them into outlaws. Everyone should have the right to choose. But that wasn't the case. They were still drilling the same message into parents' heads: "Force them to speak and they will."

Even at eleven, I was outraged by it all. And it's still going on. I have friends whose childhood was terribly hard and grueling. They can remember throwing their hearing aids down the toilet because they couldn't stand them any more. Some of those people don't talk to their parents. They just can't. I know of a little boy who became so wild and violent that he would pull his mother's hair to try to communicate with her. He would roll around on the ground, in the mud, anywhere and everywhere.

When I was in school, some of the kids would say to me, "Your mother's terrific. She can sign!" Obviously their parents didn't sign at all. Under those circumstances, what could they do to express their cares, their little problems, their feelings? How do you keep from getting upset when you can't even tell your mother about a nightmare you had, or ask her silly questions like, "What's that?" "What's that thing used for?" "Why do I hurt here?" "What's the man in the white coat with that thingamajig around his neck doing?"

How can you get by on a daily basis when nobody gives you answers or when, at best, they seem to be telling you, "Lipread. Just get what you can. Put that in your mind any which way. It doesn't matter if it takes years for you to figure it out. Speak. You have a weird voice and we don't understand you, but speak. You'll manage. Don't take off your hearing aid. Enunciate. Imitate me." In other words, "do what it takes to be like ME."

I had felt like an outsider in my own family when I was little. My classmates were having the same experience. It was over for me, but it was still going on for them. They were failing in school. To me, their failure indicated how important it was to continue the battle I was waging for LSF and how stupid it was to forbid it.

Later, I demonstrated my point in a class where the students signed among themselves (there was no way of preventing us!), but not with the teacher because that was the rule. I got a good grade in French, so the teacher called me up to the front of the class to explain the lesson to the students who hadn't understood it. I went up to the blackboard and began using sign language. The teacher stopped me cold. He accused me of being too "lax" and forced me to express myself orally. I felt ridiculous. I had never felt so ridiculous before. The students were looking at me and laughing. They weren't getting a thing out of what I was trying to say.

After what seemed an eternity, I stopped short. Not only was I miserable, but I was wasting everybody's time. I asked the teacher if he would have the "extreme kindness" of allowing me to take five minutes to say exactly the same thing all over again, but in sign language. He was convinced that I wasn't at a level advanced enough to carry it off, and that my language was limited and inferior. So he let me do it, probably thinking that it would reveal my deficiencies. The students stared at me with big smiles on their faces. Their eyes were wide open and sparkling with mischief. Usually the only times we signed to each other were to cheat, during recess, or when we were out on the street. The small revolution I had just begun was an important one. Were the students going to understand from my signing what they hadn't understood orally from the teacher?

They watched me attentively. My reasoning was clear; my explanation, convincing. The students were entranced. The teacher still refused to believe I had explained the point so quickly and so well.

"Did you understand?"

There was a unanimous "yes." He still had doubts and sardonically asked a student to come up and repeat orally what he had supposedly understood. The student did, and the teacher was dumbfounded. He looked sullen. Hiding behind his usual phoniness, he proceeded with the class orally, trying to forget what had just happened.

In my opinion, if you have a school environment where forbidding is the norm, it pits the teachers against the students. Therefore it's logical for the students to be against the teachers. As a result, we got into the habit of exchanging bits of information in sign language whenever our teacher turned around to write on the board. We were sure he wouldn't know since he wasn't looking. When we first started doing it, he'd turn around every time. That was weird. We couldn't understand how he knew. After a while, I figured out that when we used our hands to speak, we unwittingly made little noises with our mouths. So we worked at not making any sounds and, after that, it was a breeze to tell each other the answers.

Maybe it was devious, but since we generally understood only half of what was taught orally, and since it should be forbidden to forbid, we were just doing what we had to.

Chapter 12

Piano Solo

Soon I was going to be thirteen and Marie, five. She had become my alter ego, my point of reference, my sidekick. She could learn things with lightning speed. She signed with incredible energy for someone with such tiny hands and spoke with equal fluency. Marie, a little genius at five, my angel of a sister, my crutch!

From the moment she was born, I latched onto her rather possessively. But I needed her. I used her like a tool, an essential accessory. Our relationship was special.

I couldn't have grown up without her. I don't know how I would have done it alone. At the adolescent stage, kids try to get along without their parents and not ask them much. So in my case, Marie took their place. In the course of time, she became completely bilingual, signing like a real deaf person.

Deaf people have a peculiar way of making slight noises with their mouths when they sign. The sight of Marie, knee-high to a grasshopper, signing, spreading out her little fingers, and making a face with every word was sheer delight. I had priceless moments with her, even if we ended up pulling each other's hair sometimes. With her, I learned about sharing, secrets, arguments, love, and hate.

I asked her to do just about everything for me—everything I couldn't do. At mealtime, she translated the conversation. I bugged and hassled her when she would forget and leave me dangling about some detail. Sometimes she'd tell me to get lost and I either got mad or backed off, depending on the situation. There were times when we had real fights. About the phone, for example.

"Marie, make this call for me!"

"I'm sick of calling!"

"You could at least show a little concern for your deaf sister! It's easy for you. Don't let me down!"

"You're always taking advantage of me! You're using me!"

That little wisp of a five-year-old talked like a book. I was *using* her!

"Marie . . . I'm supposed to meet a friend! Come on! Call!"

And it went on like that till she agreed to do what I asked. The phone was something I loved and hated at the same time. I was jealous of people who could use it so easily. Jealous because at thirteen, you start spending a lot of time with your friends, and for deaf people, the phone means going through a hearing person. When Marie called my friends for me, sometimes their mother or father would answer. Marie was embarrassed. She didn't like having to say, "Sorry, but I'd like to talk to so-and-so. I'm calling for my sister, Emmanuelle. Please tell her . . ."

My friends' parents didn't have to know all that. Then she had to give me a rundown of the conversation. I always thought it was too short.

"Didn't they say anything else?"

"No. That's it. Her mother said she wasn't there. She'll call you back."

"But when?"

"I have no idea. You're starting to bug me!"

I got the message that she'd had enough. My requests for one thing or another were endless. If I couldn't make it somewhere, she had to call for me to let them know. If I had to change the time I was going to meet somebody, she had to make that call, too.

That was before we had our Minitel. We got it when I was fifteen. During my entire adolescence, right up until we got a Minitel, Marie was my telephone voice.

I used to tell her my secrets. Not all of them, but she knew who I was seeing or not seeing at the moment, and who I had broken up with. She took charge most of the time. She had no choice. She grew up the same time I did, almost leading two lives—mine and hers. Marie was . . . Marie. My sister. I love her.

I teased her a lot, too. Maybe it was out of jealousy. No, jealousy isn't the right word. Frustration. Marie had a relationship with my father that I couldn't have.

The piano was symbolic of that painful frustration for me. Marie began to play at an early age. Once, we were in the living room and she was playing the piano with my father. Before, I was the one who would sit at his side. I used to listen to him play and try to detect the high and low notes. Hearing aids are pretty useless for that, or anything else for that matter. But even so, I could feel Dad's music.

Now it was Marie's turn. All of a sudden, I felt excluded. They were like accomplices sharing the same encounter with that instrument. Their hands ran along the keyboard. They were smiling, tilting their heads, talking and listening to each other. It was like a love story between them. I saw the love passing through their music and it was unbearable. I ripped off my hearing aid and walked out. I couldn't take any more. She was lucky to be able to share that experience with my father. I hated that piano. I despised it.

The first time they played together, I let them know I was upset. I don't know how. After that, I would just go off to my room, alone. I was suffering from exclusion, from being different, from not being able to join my father the way she did on the same turf: music.

He was the one who had given me music. It was thanks to him that I could enjoy it, sway and dance to it. But before, music had been just for the two of us. Not any more.

Marie found out what it was like to be frustrated, too. She was still little, maybe a year old . . . I can never get the time-frame right for that period of my life. In any case, it was after we had returned from Washington. One evening, we invited Alfredo Corrado and two of his friends to the house. We were all signing at the dinner table. Everyone was deep in conversation. My parents still weren't too adept. They would make mistakes, ask for clarification, and try again. Alfredo was laughing and so was I. It was so nice to be able to speak our own language, to feel safe and secure. Suddenly, Marie climbed onto the table and started jumping up and down and stamping her feet. She was screaming and crying. Alfredo was taken aback by her display of violence, flabbergasted by the little creature's hysterical temper tantrum.

Marie just wanted to draw attention to herself. She didn't want to be ignored. She wanted everyone to remember that *she* was hearing! Our intimate conversation, so oblivious to her existence, made her furious.

How well I understood! When I was five, I was totally excluded from table conversations. All those mouths opening and closing silently, like fish in the water; all those fish going to and fro, left me high and dry on the beach. Now it was Marie's turn to be sick of language—sign language. Or just plain sick of everything. Before, they used to talk to her. Now, they signed for my benefit. Was she jealous? No, frustrated. I knew the feeling well. It was a way of reminding everybody of her identity.

I really did throw down my hearing aid when she started playing the piano with Dad. I could just as well have slammed the piano cover down. On Dad's fingers? Or Marie's? No, on the fingers of that damn piano that was talking to the people I loved and excluding me.

Piano solo. Emmanuelle solo.

Chapter *13*

Vanilla Passion

I decided to start slacking off at school. I was fed up with classes, fed up with lipreading, fed up with knocking myself out trying to produce squeaky sounds with my voice, fed up with history, geometry, and even French, fed up with disheartened teachers who did nothing but tell me off, fed up with myself and everyone else. Reality disgusted me, so I decided not to face it head on any more. I became a rebel.

Spending my life at school was ridiculous. It was like a prison and I was losing the most precious hours of my existence there. I had the impression nobody liked me. And I couldn't keep up. Everything was a waste of time.

The future was something mysterious. I didn't know what it held and didn't want to. I told myself, "Put it aside for now. Wait and see."

In the meantime, I dreamed of taking trips, countless excursions, of traveling and seeing other cultures and other people. I was dreaming of LIFE. I wouldn't listen to reason. I even wanted to have the experience of botching things. It was no use telling me, "Careful of this, careful of that . . . you'll screw up."

At thirteen, I was against the system and the way hearing people managed our deaf society. I got the feeling that I was being manipulated, that they wanted to erase my deaf identity. At school, it was as though they were saying, "You can't let your deafness show. You have to use your hearing aid and speak like hearing people. Sign language isn't pretty. It's an inferior language."

It was essentially against that kind of stupidity that my rebellion was brewing. I had heard things like that throughout my childhood, but I kept quiet. Now my anger was finally exploding.

I was thirteen when the explosion came. I was against everything. I wanted my own world, my own language. And I wanted people to leave me alone.

Deafness is the only "handicap" that isn't visible. You see people in wheelchairs, you see when someone is blind or disabled, but you don't see deafness. As a result, people have visions of eradicating it. They don't understand that deaf people really don't want to hear. They want us to be like them, with the same desires and frustrations. They want to fill a void that we don't feel exists.

I couldn't care less about hearing! I don't want to hear. I don't miss it. I don't even know what it's like to hear. You can't want something if you don't know anything about it.

I spent my time tossing my hair back, playing with my waist-length curls, tilting my head like the stars on TV, nonchalantly chewing gum and looking blasé. I would smother myself with vanilla scented perfume, to the point of making my family sick. It was my vanilla rebellion.

My body had changed. I could feel myself becoming a woman. I discovered the thrill of seduction. I discovered men. Before that, the only man in my life had been my father. Now I understood that you could have other relationships with men. Sexual relationships.

There was this guy who always used to hang around looking at me. I had my eyes on him, too. He was my vanilla passion. My spicy love, whose intense fragrance was different from those I associated with family. He was my exotic love, one that nobody had prearranged, one I had discovered by chance. It was a forbidden love, so I wanted it all the more and grabbed onto it spontaneously.

I loved my parents. I loved my family, but I needed that other kind of love. I wanted to be free of my parents' authority.

I decided not to ask them any more questions. I would ask my deaf lover instead. They spoke in terms of limits, of what was reasonable, of norms, of the right I had or didn't have to do something. But I had my own view of what my rights were.

Love isn't a right that can be prescribed. I realize now that, at thirteen, I was a little young to fall in love, but that's how it was. Romeo and

Juliet were fifteen. Mine was not a passing fancy, but rather a deep, passionate, violent love. A stubborn love that was to take up three years of my life.

Three years of *romance*. For me, romance means love and everything that goes along with it. Love of the mind, heart, and body. Passion, needing the other, complete trust. It's giving and taking, but essentially giving. I think that, when you're in love, you can give of yourself completely. But you have to learn to receive, too.

Love means surpassing yourself, trying to accept the other as he or she is, with his or her differences.

Love is vast. I loved my sister, my mother, my father. And now I loved someone else, too. He was different.

Inside Love, with a capital *L*, there are many different kinds of feelings.

I was looking for the adult kind. I had become a little adult all too fast. You might say I grew up at high speed. I went from being an overly protected child to an adolescent starved for adventure and freedom.

No, I didn't have an unhappy childhood. It wasn't horrible. I was more or less trapped, stuck, closed in, but I was essentially able to express myself, and my parents loved me. They accepted me with my difference and did everything to share it. I knew deaf children who had it much worse. They had no love, no communication. They were in an emotional desert. At thirteen, I was lucky to have the parents I did. Those other deaf kids had lost out on all counts.

My idea of rebellion was wanting to try everything, see everything, understand everything. And do it on my own.

Maybe I wanted to make up for something I had missed, but I didn't know what it was. I hadn't been deprived of love, understanding, or help. So what was it? I don't know. It was something physical. Was it a need for freedom? Independence?

My parents were worried about my rebellious behavior. All the more so because I was deaf. Especially my mother. She was afraid I might slip away from her. Afraid that I wouldn't depend on hearing people any more but on the others instead, on the deaf, and then she'd no longer have any control. In a word, that I wouldn't be safe any more.

My relationship with my father became strained. We stopped communicating. He had his problems and I had mine. The battle between us was silent, unspoken, but it was the classic father-daughter, adult-adolescent conflict. And to a certain degree, I saw it as a hearing-deaf conflict.

I was in love with a deaf boy and spending all my time with deaf people. My parents were excluded. Neither of them expected the infamous adolescent crisis to come so soon, and even less that I'd jump headlong into a love affair.

I plunged into love and my rebellion as if into the sea—with delight, undaunted by the waves and the dizzying depths swirling beneath me. I wanted HIM. He was four years older than I was, with brown hair and blue eyes. He was muscular and robust, and I liked his marginal, sort of wild side. He was deaf and signed in slang. Street talk. Was he good looking?

"He's a bit of a hood," said my mother.

That was true.

Marie said, "He's kind of a showoff."

That was true, too.

Dad said, "He's violent. Stop seeing him. He's bad company."

He was right. But I didn't stop seeing him. Instead, I talked back to my parents, "Shut up! Lay off! I love him!"

The first time we kissed was after school one day. We met secretly behind some trees in a little park, in the midst of see-saws, slides, and children's toys.

I didn't know what kissing was like. Would I like it? Would I like the taste of somebody else's mouth?

The older girls in class (they were between fifteen and sixteen) had told me about it. Deaf people ask and tell each other everything. I wanted to be as clever as they were when it came to love. I wanted to be at their level. They gave me a crash course in kissing, so I knew all about it in theory, but not in practice.

I loved HIM. Everything about HIM. I started coming home late and playing hooky. My parents knew what was going on and tried to set limits for me. But it was too late. I didn't care. I jumped over their barriers, heedless of the dangers. I wanted to discover the limits for myself, in my own way.

The most outrageous thing for me was that I felt my parents were handling the situation awkwardly at the time. They didn't pester me, but they tried to have dialog and talk with me about what was going on. On the one hand they laid down the law, yet on the other, they wanted to talk . . . and it just didn't work.

I got out of school at four o'clock and was supposed to be home by five. Little by little, I would get back at five-thirty, then six, then seven o'clock.

"Pay attention to the time. Don't get back too late. You have homework to do and school is important!" my mother would say.

"You need to let us know beforehand when you're going to come home late!" my father would say.

And I would sign back, irately, "How do you expect me to let you know? I can't pick up the phone. I'm deaf."

"You're over-dramatizing. You can always ask somebody to call for you."

"That's a pain!"

It's true, I could have. But I didn't want to. I was hiding behind my deafness to justify my need for independence. And maybe, too, so that my parents would worry. It was a way of making them understand that I wasn't feeling good about myself, that nothing was right, that looking for adventure and freedom was a way of growing up, a way of freeing myself from all those years of being completely dependent on them for everything, of freeing myself from their protective, guiding love, from talking only to them, from asking them and only them my questions.

My circle of deaf friends afforded me the freedom I was looking for. I felt at home with them. Like I was on my own planet. We would spend hours talking at the Auber metro station. It was our meeting ground, the starting place for our rebellion. In short, our home base. Our territory. The "in" spot now is the Chatelet metro station.

I kept all sorts of company—good people and not-so-good people, people who were well brought up and people who weren't brought up well at all. There were delinquents, small-time drug pushers, dealers, odd jobbers, high school friends. It was basically a teenage community with the problems typical of its age group, and deafness to boot. And we only had that one place to meet.

All those boys and girls of different ages, ethnic backgrounds, and social environments signed at breathtaking speed. We talked about movies and TV, and told each other stories or the latest gossip. We laughed and smoked, and harassed the prim and proper hearing people who went by with disapproving looks. We used to tell off passersby who stopped in surprise because they had never seen deaf people talk with their hands, gesticulate, make faces, mime, and silently roar with laughter against the racket of the screeching train wheels. We laughed at hearing guys trying to pick up girls. They hightailed it out of there as soon as we mimed, "I'm deaf, what do you want?"

We used to have parties at each other's houses with the sound system blaring, and go to nightclubs where there was loud music, booze, and pot. We literally invaded the bistros, McDonald's, and Greek restaurants. We had a pressing need to be together, with our own kind—deaf people. And we needed to be allowed to be deaf.

I ignored my parents' authority and power over me. If they had tried to lock me up, I would have scaled the wall. At the time, my rebellion and my love for my boyfriend would have prompted me to jump over all the hurdles, at the risk of my own ruin. And that almost happened.

Basically, I needed that rebellion. It was like a thirst-quenching spring. In reality, I must have loved love more than my boyfriend.

Chapter 14
Caged Seagull

I went around shouting all the time and didn't care if I pronounced words correctly or not. Yelling was my way of displaying anger. Everyone could see I was enraged. But my fury was powerless in the face of injustice and humiliation.

I was thirteen and my best friend was fifteen or sixteen. I was always the youngest in the gang.

Once there was a party at around one in the afternoon and I had promised to be back home by four. Since I had promised, I had to keep my word. I already had enough problems in that area of my life.

When it was time to leave the party, events took a strange turn. My friend had been drinking sangria and so had the two guys who were with us. I hadn't had a drop. I didn't drink when I was thirteen. By the time the four of us got on the metro, the sangria was taking effect. My friend and the two guys were laughing and acting silly. People started giving us dirty looks. As far as they were concerned, we were four young deaf people behaving badly, making too many gestures and weird faces, and laughing too much. I often noticed that people reacted that way. It was as if we frightened them.

There were some ad posters behind glass in the metro car. I don't know who started it—my girlfriend or the guys—but one of them wanted a poster and ripped it out of the frame. At the time, we just thought it was a big joke. But an old lady who had been watching us the whole time got frightened and pulled the alarm. The train came to a halt and the conductor came over.

"You can't do that!" he said.

And that was the beginning of a terrible mix-up. I tried to explain that my friend had had a little too much sangria and that it wasn't her fault. The conductor didn't understand my speech, so one of the deaf guys in our group intervened. He was pretty drunk and started telling the conductor off. So the conductor called the police and that made the two guys even madder.

There we were, the four of us, desperately trying to explain to the cops the reason for the dumb thing we had done. They refused to listen. A poster had been stolen from the metro. Our offense was visible. All they could focus on was that piece of evidence that proved our delinquent behavior. Apparently the offense is called "destruction of urban property."

They dragged us from one police station to another. Three or four in all.

I thought the whole thing was hellish, unbelievable, especially since I hadn't done anything or had anything to drink. All I wanted was to go home. Somehow, I had to explain the truth, as stupid as it was. But the guys wouldn't calm down and neither would the cops. It was getting late and I was afraid I would end up being stuck there.

Finally, when things simmered down, I tried to explain one more time where we had been, why my friends had been drinking and had gotten rowdy . . . I hadn't done anything wrong . . . hadn't had anything to drink or broken anything. I was making a concerted effort to use my voice and sign at the same time. I didn't know if they understood.

I'd had enough. I wanted them to notify my parents. They were going to get worried and I wanted them to know where I was.

"Call! . . . Call! . . ."

I was making myself hoarse imploring them. They had my ID with my name and address. I wrote my phone number on a piece of paper. Why weren't they calling? They kept nodding "yeah . . . yeah," but they still weren't calling! I don't know how many times I repeated the same thing. It drove me crazy. But it was impossible to have any dialog with those people in uniform.

They took us to another police station because of some kind of technicality that I didn't understand. Another horrific hour went by. It was seven-thirty and already dark out. The whole thing was abnormal. I was only thirteen, a minor. They didn't have the right to haul me around like that without informing my parents. I started explaining again. I was livid, sick of telling the policewoman that I hadn't done anything wrong, that it was the guys who got rowdy because they had been drinking! I felt like a panic-stricken parrot repeating the same thing for the thousandth time. It was unbelievable. And anyway, you don't throw two teenage girls in jail because of a twelve-inch poster advertising dog food, or the national lottery, or soap! I couldn't tell if she didn't understand or just didn't want to, but she was like the Berlin wall.

Another police station, and more papers. I was starting to get really frightened now. I used to think the police were the symbol of safety. Not any more. Trusting them was over for me. I was in enemy territory and scared stiff.

When they had us get into a police van, I breathed a little easier. This time they were going to take me home. Everything would get straightened out. But instead, the van pulled up to a jail. A real jail, with an iron gate and walls!

I refused to get out. I didn't want to go in. If they locked me up, I'd never get out!

The guys weren't with us any more. They had been taken somewhere else. My friend and I were alone, looking at each other, frightened, and signing frantically:

"They didn't call!"

"They don't want to!"

"They're going to lock us up!"

"I don't want to get out of the van!"

I became hysterical. Choking with anger, I screamed, "Call my parents! They'll be worried! Please, think about them! You have to call!"

"Pipe down!" snapped a cop.

That seemed like a real threat. So now I didn't have the right to express myself any more.

They forced us out, and we went through the prison entrance. A nun was waiting at the door. We followed her in. The whole episode was so crazy, so unfair.

What was I guilty of? Of wanting to explain? Of what the others had done? I felt like injustice was closing in on me, like I was getting the raw end of the deal. It was disgusting. What they were doing to me was horrible.

We went into a room where a woman told us to remove our shoelaces and take off our bracelets. She put everything in two small plastic bags.

"Why are you doing that?"

"Suicide. You can hang yourself with a shoestring."

Those words sent another shockwave through me. I was overcome with anguish. I felt the deepest, darkest distress. I was really in prison, like a criminal. They were taking away my laces the way they did with murderers!

It reeked of bleakness, hopelessness, and death in there. And my parents didn't know a thing about what was going on. They must have been thinking that I had disobeyed and was still hanging around at the party or with my boyfriend. They had no idea where to call, what deaf person to contact to ask, "Where's Emmanuelle?" And besides, nobody would have been able to tell them anything anyway.

The woman offered us something to eat—an egg and a tomato. I wasn't hungry and neither was my friend. So they took us into a huge room with a staircase in the middle leading to cells on either side. The nun led the way, holding an enormous set of keys. There were other rooms full of girls. I wondered if she was showing us all that to frighten us. She opened the door of a dimly lit cell and pushed me in, alone.

"I want to sleep with my friend!"

She refused. She wanted to separate us. So I started screaming, and screaming, and screaming, like a seagull wailing in a storm. I couldn't take being locked up alone in there! I wanted my friend. I was too afraid. There was no way I could spend the entire night surrounded by those disgusting walls without her, with no one to talk to! I screamed so much that the nun gave in.

Slam! We were both locked up. There were iron bunk beds with no sheets, but some sort of gray blankets folded in four. There was just a hole in the floor for the toilet and a grungy sink. Revolting. We huddled up against each other, glued together with fright.

What was going to happen? They hadn't told us a thing. How long would we have to stay there? What about our parents? Where were we?

It was a nightmare. We were truly panic-stricken. Both of us were terrified at being locked up, even though we were together. Why this injustice? Why couldn't we get our message across? Why wouldn't they call our parents? What did they want from us? We felt humiliated, like outcasts, wretches. Outraged and terrified. Full of hopelessness and dejection.

It stank in that dump. The night crept along in black silence. What could we do? Start banging on things or kicking the blasted door? They didn't give a damn about us, and hadn't from the very beginning.

Start screaming again? I was too tired. Exhausted, mixed-up, lost. I didn't even know where I was. Which prison? I had a sneaking suspicion

I'd spend the rest of my life there, that no one would come get me out because no one could hear me and they would never notify my parents. It was illegal detention. We were the hearing cops' hostages and they despised us. They realized we were deaf. They had seen me implore them. They had my ID. They knew how old I was. Even if they thought I had committed a heinous crime, they didn't have the right to withhold information from my parents! They had locked us up like vicious dogs! Like mangy animals you don't talk to, that you kick and drag around, and tell to "Shut up!"

I hated them. They frightened me and I hated them.

In the middle of the night, we fell asleep from exhaustion. Two women woke us up in the morning. Again, I started explaining that I hadn't done anything and that I wanted them to call my parents. The woman still wouldn't listen. She was just interested in putting my hands behind my back to handcuff me! So now they were handcuffing me! Tying me up and still not listening to me!

Outside, they shoved us into a police van with our hands behind our backs. Where were we going? They were talking to each other, but I couldn't understand what they were saying. They took us to another police station and started all over with the same routine. And I did what I had done the night before—explained and explained till I was out of breath, till my throat was sore and my mouth twisted out of shape.

"Call my parents . . . "

And suddenly that was it. My fear changed to anger. I had had it with their nodding at me as though I were some kind of moron. I shouted, "I'm sick of your saying yes! Enough is enough!"

Then I grabbed the phone from under the nose of that stupid woman and, still screaming, dialed the number. I held out the receiver to her, forced it to her ear. I was so sick of it all, I had tears in my eyes.

"Talk . . . Please, talk . . ."

I glared at her. It worked. She started talking. She was talking to someone at my house. After what seemed a very short time, she hung up. I figured out that she had spoken to my father and that he was going to come. At last!

The tightness in my throat started to loosen up and my anger subsided. But what about my friend? Her parents were deaf. How could they be notified? Dad would take care of that.

We were in a police station for minors, and there were a lot of teenagers there. I tried talking to a girl who was waiting around like us. She managed to explain to me that she had run away. I told her the story about the sangria, the poster, and the metro. Then her mother showed up. She was really mad and had a scowl on her face. She talked with the cops but her daughter didn't say anything. She just waited. Suddenly, her mother smacked her. I could see the girl's nose was bleeding.

Was my father going to hit me, too? My parents never hit me but, in a situation like this, the same thing could very well happen to me. Why did her mother hit her? It wasn't logical. I couldn't understand it. I had no idea violence like that existed between mothers and daughters.

It was beyond me. I couldn't think rationally. I was really afraid my father was going to slap me when he got there. But instead, he took me in his arms and I cried my eyes out.

Then I explained what had happened. Everything, the sangria, the metro, the poster, the night in jail, the cops who wouldn't call, the damn phone!

Naturally, my parents were terribly worried. They were about to call the police when I finally got to the damn phone. My father was furious, appalled. He demanded an explanation. But the cops just kept parading back and forth, saying things like, "I'm not responsible for notifying parents of minors. I only accompany them . . .", "Oh! That's not my job. I transfer minors, but they don't tell me why!"

Dad was furious! He started yelling at the cops. He wanted to file a complaint, call a lawyer, and let the press know. But he didn't because my little sister Marie had been in a serious car accident and was in the hospital. My parents were with her every day. My father wanted to take my friend with us. Her deaf parents still hadn't been told. The cop refused, "No! Her parents have to come down to the station!"

"But how are you going to notify them?"

"No problem. We'll take care of it. You can't take her. You're not her father."

There was nothing we could do. We felt bad leaving her there. The poor girl told me later that she had to wait around in the station till the end of the day before her parents came. The police had to call a neighbor who contacted somebody else, or something like that. It took another whole day before the police finally let her parents know!

The guys were sent to jail, but they felt sort of guilty. It didn't affect them the way it did me. I had a rough time with the whole experience. It was the same battle whether with cops or hearing people. I was thirteen and already in a state of rebellion, so this just hardened me all the more. What I needed right then was a positive, reassuring image of the police and the society they represented . . . hearing people.

The contempt they displayed left an indelible mark on me. I never forgot it. I couldn't trust anyone any more after that. There was their world and mine. In their world, they put me in jail and refused to talk to me. They made no attempt to communicate. It was as though the wall I felt in my childhood had just been put back up. The experience of being locked up was like a horror film and now my imagination was limitless. I wondered what the cops would come up with next, what they were going to do to us. They were plotting something horrible and maybe my parents would never find me. I was isolated again, unable to communicate. But on top of that, the whole thing was humiliating and I knew it, even at that age.

When I think back on that episode and the terrible sensation of injustice it provoked in me, when I think about their contempt for me, it still makes me cringe. I needed my mother or father that day. It was my right. I needed for somebody to listen. That was my right, too.

Instead, they pushed me further into my loneliness, back to when I had to tug at my mother's sleeve so that she'd listen to me, to the time when the slightest furrow on my father's brow, the slightest hint of anger worried me. The time when the hearing world was a huge mystery, a bundle of incomprehensible things, a dangerous and unknown planet.

If I had been allowed to speak at my own pace, if I had been respected for the person I was, then all those misunderstandings and injustices might never have happened. Maybe my rebellion would have settled down and I would have never done the stupid things I did later on, which were far worse. Just maybe.

After the trauma was over, I tried to explain what I felt to my parents. But not right away because I was so shaken up. At one point, I told them about it in general terms, but it was impossible to convey the emotions I was experiencing, everything I was feeling so intensely. It was as though my young soul had been raped. That's really the impression I had. My perception of the world, my vision of it, had been violated. All notions of protection, security, and confidence were destroyed. Torn apart. But I couldn't find the words to express it at the time. Now I say "raped" and "torn," but I don't know if those are the right words. I don't think they're strong enough. My parents most likely didn't understand the violent emotions I was feeling inside—suffering, humiliation, injustice, and rage. The police had misjudged me. I had been taken for a moron who just experienced things without understanding them. I could see the cops' disdain in their behavior. That hurt me terribly.

I was screaming behind bars at people who chose not to hear me. I couldn't get past that situation and find any sort of reassurance. Injustice is a terrible thing. When you're in jail, you have no choice but to shut up and do as you're told. I've never felt such intense suffering as that.

One question stuck in my mind: How do people understand each other with their backs turned? I can only understand if we're looking at each other.

I used to have fun and laugh a lot with my father, but were we really communicating? When I tried to talk to him, he didn't always understand what I wanted to say. And he felt bad about that.

The way my mother and I communicated was instinctive, animal-like, what I call "umbilical." We had signs that were our very own, completely made up.

In this picture, I'm playing *barbichette*, a children's game. You try to make the other players laugh and, if you succeed, you get to hit them. I'm not happy because my mother won and gave me a little tap.

I was the only deaf child in kindergarten class. I felt isolated.

When I was seven, two treasures came into my life: French Sign Language (LSF) and my little sister, Marie.

I started opening up and discovering the world. In sign language, my name is Sun-Coming-from-the-Heart.

My first class with deaf children. I finally had friends!

One evening, my Uncle Fifou, a musician, told me to bite the neck of his guitar. I kept on biting it for hours while he played. The music started singing inside me. After that, I insisted on having a guitar.

On vacation at
my paternal
grandparents'.

When I was nine, I did some theater work at the International
Visual Theater in Vincennes, where I learned sign language.
This play was called *Journey to the End of the Metro*.

Deaf people demonstrating for the recognition of
French Sign Language.

In 1986, I was
already an
activist!

At sixteen, I had trouble reconciling the deaf and hearing worlds. I was going through a rebellious stage and everything seemed hard to me.

Fortunately, there were some good times!

. . . like this play, *Day and Night* that I did with Claire Garguier in the metro!

After I finished my baccalaureate exam, I worked with Jean Dalric, who helped me get into hearing theater. We're rehearsing *Children of a Lesser God.*

Photo J.-F. Roussier / Sipa Press.

With members of the *Children of a Lesser God* production (*back row, left to right*): Fanny Druilhe (deaf), Jean Dalric, Joël Chalude (deaf), Anie Balestra; (*front row*): Daniel Bremont, and Nadine Basile.

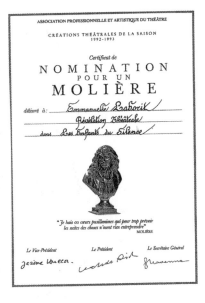

Poster for *Children of a Lesser God*. The
sign signifies the joining of two worlds.

Emotion

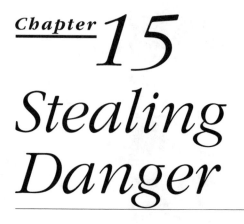

Chapter 15
Stealing Danger

We got a Minitel! It was like a magic invention. Now I could talk to people on the phone without going through an intermediary. I cried for joy because it meant I would be more independent. Finally, at fifteen, I had discovered a gold mine of freedom.

The Minitel let me communicate with my friends on my own by typing my message and sending it electronically. It was a godsend and a real liberation!

My parents planned the whole thing as a surprise. When I first saw it, it looked like some sort of small typewriter with a television screen, connected to the phone. My mother had already set it up, so all I had to do was plug it in. My friend Claire called me. The Minitel started flashing and I saw Claire's message appear on the screen. My father, mother, and Marie were all watching me. I was choked with emotion. At last I was independent!

Now I didn't need to pester my sister any more to call Claire. We talked for hours. She was even more talkative than I was and we could easily blab on the Minitel for an hour or two telling each other our life stories. It was great for both of us, but it was expensive. And a bit risky when you're fifteen and have secrets you don't want your parents to know about.

It was because of a friend of mine that one of my secrets got found out. Spying on me was the furthest thing from my mother's mind, but one day while I was out, she happened to notice a disturbing message on the Minitel screen: "Hi Emmanuelle! Are you still sick?"

When I got home that evening, my mother and I locked horns.

"So you've been sick, have you?"

I tried to lie, but she stopped me dead in my tracks. The truth was that I had been cutting classes, and my mother had no intention of letting the matter drop. We had a violent argument in sign language. My mother was yelling the whole time, which of course served no purpose.

"There's no point in screaming. I'm deaf!" I signed.

That just made her madder because she knew I was only being facetious. Yes I was deaf, but I was also a liar. The fight escalated to the point where Marie became terrified and ran to her room crying. A little later, I was the one crying in my room. Then Marie came in and we cried some more together.

Everything was a big deal for me during that period of my life, especially the fact that my parents couldn't accept the affair I was having with my deaf boyfriend. They were frightened by our intense, violent relationship. He was older than I was, and a loner. He skipped classes, dealt in who knows what, often got into fights, and always had his fists out ready for action. He was possessive and demanding. And I trusted him blindly. He was my *tough guy*. They knew enough to be afraid of him, but I didn't. We were so attracted to each other that nothing between us was clear-cut except our mutual attraction. I didn't stop one minute to think about what might be wrong with him, why he was so violent, why he was a loner, and why he always overreacted. I thought I knew him better than anyone else because I loved him. He wasn't lucky enough to have parents like mine. He was looking for love, the way I was. He wanted me and I wanted him. I was so completely enveloped in that personal and slightly insane adventure that I refused to listen to anyone or anything. Maybe he was screwed up. So what! I loved him. Period. That was it.

Besides, he wasn't really the reason why I was cutting classes. It was the oral method that kept me away, the feeling that I was losing precious time. I wanted to live my life.

That evening, the heated argument continued. My father took up where my mother had left off. This time, my heart sank as I listened to him without saying a word.

I promised never to cut classes again and I kept my promise. But Emmanuelle Laborit had decided she wouldn't pay attention in school any more. She would be present physically but she would be mentally absent from class. My behavior irritated the teachers. They couldn't pierce the bubble I had created around myself and that protected me from their smirks. Talk all you want, I won't retain a thing. And if you ask me to open my mouth, I'll only do it to deride you, or to talk to my classmates, but not to learn what you're trying to force down my throat.

That was the year of living dangerously. I committed every foolish extravagance imaginable, and learned everything there was to learn. It was also the year I became politically involved. I took part in demonstrations for the recognition of sign language because I felt it was something positive and constructive. I wanted deaf people to be informed. I wanted to be an activist. I wanted them to stop banning my language. I wanted deaf children to have the right to a full education, and I wanted them to have a bilingual school. It was absolutely essential to promote sign language in France and not just teach it to an elite minority. They had to stop banning it. On that point, my mother didn't interfere: "If it's important to you, then do it."

My parents were already fairly permissive, but unfortunately, I took advantage of that. They had no idea what I was up to and only found out through the grapevine that I was hanging out with my friends at the Auber metro station. That was home base for the deaf at the time, our little ghetto where we would tell each other everything, gossip, and make plans together. Hearing teenagers did the same thing in other places—on the outskirts of the city, in vacant lots, or the grounds of apartment buildings.

The big difference between the two groups is that when one deaf person meets another for the first time, they talk about themselves. It's a deaf thing. They tell each other the story of their lives. And they do it on the spot, as though they had always known each other. The dialog is instantaneous, straightforward, and easygoing. It's not at all like hearing people's conversations. Hearing people don't jump right into it the first time they meet. Getting to know each other is a slow, careful process. It takes time for them to get acquainted. And loads of words to get to that point. They have their own way of thinking, of constructing their ideas, and it's different from mine, or rather ours.

Hearing people begin their sentences with a subject. Then comes a verb, an object, and finally, at the very end, the idea. For example, "I decided to go to a restaurant and have some oysters." (I love oysters.)

In sign language, the main idea comes first, then possibly some details and the sentence's context. Since eating is the main objective in the example I just gave, it would be the first sign in the sentence. If I wanted to add details, I could go on for hours. It seems I'm as fond of details as I am oysters.

What's more, everybody has a particular way of signing, or signing style, sort of the way everybody's voice is different. Some people go on forever and others take shortcuts. Some sign in slang, others more traditionally. But it only takes a few seconds for deaf people to get to know each other.

Actually, we already know each other. "You're deaf? So am I." And we're off. The feeling of solidarity is immediate, like between two tourists in a foreign country. And our conversation goes right to the heart of the matter: "What do you do? Who do you like? Who do you hang out with? What do you think about so-and-so? Where are you going tonight?"

Communication with my mother is frank and direct, too. She's not like hearing people who hide behind words, only saying things superficially.

Upbringing, conventions, words that aren't said, words that are implied, avoided, vulgar, taboo. Artificial words. Unspoken words. Words that are like shields.

There are no signs that are prohibited, hidden, implied, or vulgar. Signs are direct and simply mean what they represent. Hearing people might sometimes find them blunt.

When I was little, for example, it would have been unthinkable to forbid me to point at something or someone! I was never told, "Don't do that. It's impolite!"

Pointing my finger at someone or picking up an object was already my way of communicating. There was no gestural behavior forbidden me. Conveying hunger, thirst, or a stomachache is visible. When you like or dislike something, that's visible, too. Some people might feel uneasy with that kind of visibility, with such a lack of conventional restrictions.

At thirteen, I had decided I didn't want any more taboos, regardless of where they came from. It was a blow to my parents but they dealt with it as best they could. At the Auber metro, I was at home, free, in my own community.

But when you hop on the back of a metro car and speed off like the wind from station to station, playing Tarzan and Jane, you can get killed. I never told anyone, but that's something I did. Sorry, Mom and Dad. Luckily, I survived. It was one of my life-learning experiences. There was no holding me back, till fortunately somebody or something prevented me from going any further.

I always attended the functions organized by the French anti-racist group SOS Racism with my deaf and hearing friends. One night, after dancing and making conversation with whoever happened to be there, we decided to take the metro. It was around one A.M. The cars were packed, and everyone was squeezing up against each other. A tall black guy who couldn't get on gestured to me laughingly to come join him between the two cars and hold onto the door handle on the outside. I thought it was a fun idea and so, instead of piling in with all the others, I did it.

I was afraid, really afraid, but it was an exhilarating fear. The stations went whizzing by one after the other, and at each stop I was convinced I wouldn't have the guts to make it to the next one. But I held on. I made it a point of pride not to give up and bravely counted to the last stop, playing the hero to the end. It was totally crazy.

I never bragged about the incident. Now when I look back on it, it scares me. Maybe the trains at the Auber station still remember.

We were in an oral school all day long. So as soon as we got out, we desperately needed to recover from the ordeal, to just be together and talk. Not only did we have to make up for the time we lost being with hearing people all day, but we had to get our language and identity back as well. We wouldn't have felt that way if sign language had been allowed in school. We wouldn't have been in a ghetto. If there hadn't been so much frustration and censorship, everything would have been much simpler. But nothing was easy for us. After spending the day understanding no more than about half of what the teacher was saying, all we wanted to do was talk on and on, and do things as a group. Being together was important, but that was when we'd do stupid things.

I was around fifteen or sixteen and wanted a good-looking pair of jeans. All the girls my age dreamed about clothes. And jeans were the "in" thing. Not the ugly cheap kind you could get on sale, but the super cool designer type. The ones that cost at least four hundred francs.

But my parents weren't very rich. I was already maxing them out with the Minitel, my classes, and all the rest. There was no way I was going to ask them for spending money on top of all that. My pride made me commit THE biggest blunder of all. This time there was no excuse. I was guilty from the start. My friend and I were both guilty.

We decided to each swipe a pair of jeans from a department store. Levi's. The expensive ones.

There we were in the clothing department looking for our size. We managed to pry the magnetic detection device off the bottom of the jeans in the fitting room. Then we looked all around and went out with the jeans inconspicuously jammed in a bag. The saleslady in charge of the fitting rooms wasn't there. We went down the stairs with our eyes peeled. But when I looked behind, I noticed she was watching us from far away and talking to a woman in plain clothes.

I signed to my friend, "She's watching us. I'm sure she's looking at us."

"No she's not. Don't worry. You're imagining it. It's okay."

"She looks serious! I'm sure we've been spotted."

"Knock it off. You're paranoid!"

We got off the escalator, crossed the main floor and started going out the door. We were ecstatic. We had almost made it.

All of a sudden, I felt myself being grabbed from behind. The woman pulled my hands behind me and led me back into the store.

"Whatever you do, don't talk! Don't make a sound," my friend quickly signed to me.

I did as she said. Neither of us uttered a word. All communication stopped. It was our only defense . . . an instinctive reaction. The deaf refuge. But my brain was working like crazy. They're going to call my parents. This is horrible. I'm a thief.

They took us down to the police station. The woman emptied our bags. We just looked at her and didn't say anything. She asked me for an ID but I pretended I didn't understand.

She tried to explain by gesturing and showing me papers. She realized we were deaf. She had clearly seen us signing to each other, but there was absolutely no way we were going to talk now. That was the only thing we could do to confuse the issue. They looked for our names in our notebooks but struck out on that one because I didn't write my name in my notebooks (I was a big girl, in high school, not kindergarten). But my friend did, so they got her name. But nothing else.

Then they searched us. A pushy policewoman manhandled us like rag dolls. I could tell tension was mounting. On top of it all, I couldn't stand the way she was pawing us. I started screaming, pretending to talk in broken speech. I was perfectly capable of constructing a correct sentence but, instead, just yelled any old thing in her face. She had really angered me, poking and feeling me with her dirty paws the way she did. To my surprise, she tried to calm me down. Then a man came in to take our statements. He sat down and said, "What you did was bad. Keep it up and you'll wind up in jail."

I nodded yes, yes, like a little girl.

"Go on! Get out of here!"

At first, I didn't believe it. I said to myself, "Careful, it's a trap. They're doing it on purpose."

But no, the man said it again and gestured for us to go: "Scram!"

We picked up our bags and started to leave, making sure not to run. Our backs were stiff. We were still worried. But it was true, they were letting us go!

When we got out onto the street, we jumped for joy. We laughed nervously, uncontrollably, because we were so scared. And we cried at the same time. We kept going over how we had tricked them, adding more and more details: how afraid we were, how they had searched us, the gesturing, my screaming, and then how they had let us go!

I went home. I had learned my lesson. Never again. I never stole anything ever again. If that woman hadn't spotted me, maybe I would have kept on doing it out of bravado. But getting caught, plus the fear, and shame if my parents had found out, made me realize what I was doing. I felt guilty and accountable. Well, let's say a bit guilty and a bit accountable.

I was no little saint. I was difficult, tough, quarrelsome, rebellious. I had to experience things for myself head on, and then decide if I wanted to keep doing them or not.

As for stealing, that was over. Once was enough.

Mouette the thief.

Chapter 16
Smooth as Silk

Mothers have cat eyes and I don't know what kind of ears. It was useless tiptoeing in at dawn; mine was already awake.

"Is everything all right? Did you get home okay? Any problems?"

"Everything's okay, Mom. Go to sleep. Everything's all right. Go to bed."

It's easy to say everything's okay. But you obviously run risks coming home at four A.M.

One time, after leaving a nightclub, I got into a cab to go home. When we were stopped at a red light, the driver turned to me and asked, "Want to go to a hotel?"

Who did he think I was? In any case, I must have looked surprised because he kept on, and craned his neck so he could see me.

"Don't worry. I'll pay you!" he added.

It was a tricky situation, not really scary, but still . . . I tried to stall for time and outsmart him as best I could, "Besides, I'm deaf. You can't do that to me! Don't you feel sorry for me?"

The light turned green, but the cab didn't move. He tried again. I didn't understand the whole sentence, but the idea was clear enough. I started to get a little angry, "Get going, the meter's running. Let's get moving here. This is costing me."

There was a moment of silence and then he said, gruffly, "Either we go to a hotel or you get out here!"

I got out. I slammed the door and started looking for another cab, still thinking about the way the driver had acted. He had been aggressive and violent. It shocks me to this day. It makes me mad. He could have at least asked me, given me a choice! "Do you want to or not?" I don't want to, so let's not talk about it any more. But no. I'm still relieved he wasn't a rapist.

There were other situations like that, ranging from basically harmless to incredibly traumatic. For example, I've been propositioned by guys just trying to pick up girls on the street. They think I won't scream because I'm deaf. Lots of times, people think that when you're deaf you're mute, too. But I'm not mute. Mouette isn't mute. A man was following me once and I couldn't shake him off. I started getting worried, so I used my hands and my voice to yell in both languages. I let out a good scream, one that could be heard, and he beat it out of there fast.

I had an even more disturbing experience but I didn't scream that time. I couldn't. I decided it would be better not to for my own safety. Yet the incident was both distressing and shocking.

As usual, I was running late and hopped on the metro elevator. I just made it before the door closed. My thoughts were somewhere else. I needed to think up an excuse to give my parents for being late. That was when we were having horrible arguments. They tried everything in their power to spook me out so I would stop behaving like a social misfit. From the time I was thirteen right up to age seventeen, they were constantly on my back about all the shenanigans I had already pulled, was pulling, and was still going to pull. I refused to take any advice. In fact, I usually did the exact opposite of what they told me. It got to the point where they couldn't take it any more. They were at a complete loss. They bickered a lot, and even talked about getting a divorce.

But that didn't change the way I was acting. On the contrary, I got worse. That night, I stayed out really late at a bistro, talking with some older deaf friends. They could stay out longer, but it was past my time to go home so I had to get back. To make a long story short, I ended up in the metro elevator all alone with some young guy.

Metro elevators can be pretty spooky. They're metallic and eerie. The heavy doors closed slowly. The guy came up to me and started talking. I put a finger over my mouth and on my ear, meaning, "Can't speak. Can't hear." And I didn't say a word. I gestured because I didn't feel like talking. That's the usual way of putting up a wall between myself and other people so they'll leave me alone. The guy looked suspicious to me.

He kept on talking. I shook my head to say I didn't understand. Then he pulled down his pants and masturbated in front of me.

Being stuck there in front of that disgusting display was torture. Every time I looked away, he moved in front of me so I would have to watch. It made me sick. I was scared to close my eyes because I thought, if I did, he might attack me. My eyes are my ears, my only resource. Without them, I can't confront danger.

I was seized with panic and wondered if I should scream or not. The elevator was dreadfully slow. If I screamed, he might get violent. So I gritted my teeth and concentrated, keeping my eyes open to give him the impression I was calm, deaf, and incapable of screaming. That's probably what he was thinking. It must have put him at ease to think he could attack someone who was defenseless, and couldn't yell, "You pervert!" But inside my head, everything was spinning around. I was on the verge of hysteria. Electrified, ready to explode. Yet I held onto the one slim hope left: Keep still. Don't scream. If you do, he'll jam the elevator and rape you. Keep still. Keep still.

He finished his business just as the elevator stopped. It was sickening. Revolting. Enough to make you nauseous. Then he said, "Thank you very much," and calmly got off the elevator.

I was shocked. Bewildered. The incident escaped my understanding. What did that guy want? Was that all? Did he do it because he knew I was deaf? Or because he was just plain sick? I was only sixteen and that type of sexual assault totally baffled me. When I got home, I told my mother what had happened.

"You were lucky. He might have been dangerous."

I couldn't have stood it if he had touched me. That's what I was afraid of. I would have put up a fight if necessary. When I was sixteen, I used to practice a type of boxing called *savate*. Not to defend myself, but because it was graceful, aesthetic, and I liked it. I knew exactly where a blow from the knee would really hurt a man. If something like that happened to me today, I'd still have the reflexes to poke his eyes with my fingers or kick him in the right place with my knee. I only get violent and aggressive when people touch me. Luckily, that has never happened.

After the elevator incident, my mother bought me a can of mace so I could protect myself if someone tried to assault me. But that didn't stop me from going to night clubs and coming home late at night.

A few weeks later, when I was taking an elevator again, a man came up to me. I immediately started yelling, "Don't touch me! Don't touch me!" And I got out as quickly as I could. Maybe he just wanted to ask me the time, but I was so traumatized by the last experience that I decided not to take any chances.

I wasn't afraid of much of anything then. A rough situation like the one in the elevator was stressful at the time, but hearing girls got attacked, too. You have to get a hold of yourself, control your reactions, decide whether or not you should scream. I don't think only deaf people like me are victims of that kind of assault. I was taking the same risks that a hearing girl as rebellious, obstinate, and strong-minded as myself might. In any case, I didn't want to be thought of as someone who had to be constantly protected.

At that age, when you're going through a full-blown identity crisis, you scoff at danger till one day you find yourself staring at it right in the face. Because I never like to do things half way, I always felt I had to outdo myself and was ready to accept the consequences of my actions. I was basically a normal, independent individual, with my own identity. As my mother put it, "Emmanuelle refuses to be considered handicapped."

That's right. As far as I'm concerned, sign language is my voice and my eyes are my ears. Frankly, I don't feel deprived of anything. It's society that makes me handicapped, that makes me dependent on hearing people, that makes it impossible to contact a doctor directly, that makes me need to have conversations translated, that makes me have to ask for help to make a phone call or for captioning on TV (there are so few captioned programs). With more Minitels and captioning, I, or rather we, the deaf, could have better access to culture. There wouldn't be a handicap, a deadlock, a border between us any more.

The focus of my rebellion had changed. When I was thirteen, I was concerned with not being dependent on my parents or having to be accountable to them. Deaf kids are necessarily more dependent on their parents than hearing kids are. I wanted to get away from that. But I especially wanted to get away from the oral teaching method. The education they were forcing on me had become agonizing. My life was being swallowed up. Now that I was sixteen, my rebellion took a different course. I had evolved and other things bothered me. My relationship with my father was practically nonexistent. The only time he talked to me was to reprimand me:

"You go out too much. You don't do anything any more. You're seeing dangerous people. You're screwing up your future. You have to stop."

That was the extent of the conversations between us. I could tell
my mother was constantly concerned, even though she didn't say anything.
She tried to go along with my antics and hassle me as little as possible, but
I could clearly see she was worried. Marie was a brilliant student then, always at the head of her class. She was very gifted, and sometimes nearly
outdid me. We were always partners, sisterly friends, never enemies except
for the normal friction, and that didn't last long. Fortunately, communication between us never broke down.

What worried me most was seeing my parents talk more and more
about divorce. The day I realized they were really going to separate, I guess
I accepted the fact. It was one of those times when life's urgency takes
precedence over everything else. I did my best to rationalize their splitting
up. But I was suffering and imagined the worst. I was afraid they would ask
me to choose between them. Between two loves. That didn't happen. After my parents got divorced, I lived with both of them.

I would trade off on Wednesdays or weekends. Saturday night, I
would tell my mother, "I'm letting you know now that I'm going to a night
club and I'll be home late." Another Saturday, I'd tell my father the same
thing. The only difference was that my father slept like a log and didn't hear
me come home. He's a sound sleeper.

At any rate, I felt incapable of stitching the threads of my childhood
back together. My first thought was that they were getting divorced because
of me, because of my lack of discipline and my wild behavior. Maybe even
because I had been born deaf.

Actually, I didn't know anything about the reasons for the divorce.
That was their business. My mother was quick to reassure me. She didn't
want me to feel guilty. No one was to blame, not even me. I would be able
to keep my love for both of them intact. That was important because affection has always been at the heart of my high-spiritedness and my rebellious attitude. I think I could have accepted everything in life, the way I
finally accepted my parents' divorce, if the people who tried to force things
on me had done it with feeling.

My oralist teachers didn't know about the divorce and neither did
my boyfriend. My parents' divorce was like a wound that just wouldn't heal.
I accepted it, but getting over it was a slow process so it was important for

me not to be left alone. When people get divorced, their children spend their time going back and forth between them, weekend after weekend.

At that stage of my life, I clung to the tumultuous, all-encompassing passion I shared with my lover. I trusted him implicitly. Trust was important to me. Later, I realized I had made a mistake. But I won't talk about that yet because I've decided to write my memoirs in chronological order; I'll save it for later. At sixteen, I was still caught in the web of a love affair that had gone adrift. At school, I was so far behind that my prospects for the future were being jeopardized. And besides, I was still determined not to give a damn about my future.

On Fridays, my gang used to get together at McDonald's. We would meet upstairs and talk for hours, kind of like at a private club. It was more comfortable than the metro, and we really didn't know where else to go. We would get there at six and could easily spend three hours together. We'd buy a hamburger, a Coke or some coffee, and settle in. We basically camped out there.

The owner didn't like it very much. I don't think it was because there weren't enough seats for the customers. There were tables available all around us and there was never much of a crowd between six and nine. I guess he didn't like the fact that our deaf gang had decided to congregate at *his* McDonald's.

One of the employees always came over and asked us to leave. But we refused. He'd go off somewhere, then come back a little later, and the whole thing would start all over. One night, the boss came up to our table. He was downright mad.

"Get out of here! Split! Clear out!"

A deaf friend across from me explained in sign language that he had the right to stay there because he was eating. The boss wouldn't listen.

"You're not staying! Clear out! You have two seconds to beat it out of here!"

He was treating him like a dog. I couldn't take it. I broke in and said in French, "Excuse me, but can we talk about this? We're not dogs. We're human beings!"

I have no idea whether he understood or not. Sometimes my spoken "accent" is hard to understand, especially when I'm angry, which was the case. In any event, he must have understood what I meant from the tone of my voice, but he refused to talk about it.

"No way! Clear out!"

I could tell a fight was brewing. My nerves were jumping and I wanted to let him have it. But he wouldn't listen to me. He was just one more hearing person refusing to listen. I wanted to at least explain to him that we were there because all day long we felt frustrated in a world that wasn't our own. We needed to be together. The restaurant was empty downstairs, and we weren't taking anyone's seat. We were sorry. If we had to buy another Coke or hamburger, we would. I wanted to explain that we could reach a compromise and talk about it. But he refused to listen or try to understand us. Then a friend signed to me, "Drop it. Let's go."

Anyway, we were used to being kicked out of places. Like other teenagers. We kept changing locations all the time, looking for a friendly spot, but generally they would politely throw us out. This was the first time they were so vicious about it though. We were human beings and that man talked to us the way you would to a dog. I'm sure he would have had more compassion for a pack of mutts from the SPCA.

I can sympathize with him. It was a nuisance having a bunch of teenagers in his establishment. It disrupted his routine, and he didn't need the hassle. But to take the tone he did with us! And to be so obnoxious! Maybe he couldn't communicate with me, but that wasn't the real problem. He could have at least tried.

I looked at him with real anger. Mouette was infuriated. He lowered his voice and said, "All right, but don't stay too long."

We finally left in disgust. When I got home, I told my mother, "If that's what communicating with hearing people is like, I don't want to have anything to do with it."

She tried to calm me down, but I was outraged. In reality, my anger was a cover-up for my suffering. I told myself, "It's revolting. You can't change the world by snapping your fingers."

The incident might seem anecdotal, but I'm always angered by the ever resurfacing conflict between deaf and hearing people, especially when there's a group of us. I believe wholeheartedly that dialog between the two worlds and cultures is possible. I live with hearing people. I communicate with them. I live with deaf people, and I communicate with them even better. It's only natural. But we're the ones who always have to go out of our way. That's what I feel personally, in any case. But I keep at it. I'm still trying. I would like to see harmony among the deaf and hearing. I'd like to see the wall of distrust crumble. But I haven't made it happen yet.

I've been able to enjoy that kind of trust with my mother and sister, as well as other hearing people. I don't mean to generalize or sound like a defeatist, but maybe the ideal I'm striving for isn't possible. It depends on an individual's personality, upbringing, and education.

I don't have the fits of anger I had when I was sixteen any more. As a matter of fact, I sometimes discuss the issue with deaf people. It's often our favorite topic of conversation. Some are hard-nosed extremists who say, "We want a promised land, a country for deaf people. We'll never be able to live with hearing people!" Those types close themselves off from the world. I understand their reaction, but suggest they take it easy with demands like that. They need to think more and open themselves up to others. I reject extremism from either side. But maybe I've been unusually fortunate in my social dealings.

Oftentimes, I escape into my own world. I can't always be the one asking the questions, so I consciously exclude myself and start to daydream. Sometimes people forget about me, but it isn't their fault. When I think about a situation that aggravates me or about people who don't make any effort to communicate, here's what I ask myself, "Could I fit in with people like that on a daily basis? Could I live without deaf people around me?" I need deaf people. I also need hearing people, and anyway I can't wipe them off the map. I go from one world to the other.

Spending a whole month only with hearing people is tough. It's constant work. You begin to wonder how long you'll be able to hold out. The difference is there. It's unavoidable. You reach a point when you really need to see deaf people. I tried it once in Spain with my parents. By the end of the month, I was miserable. I felt stifled. I was at my outer limit. Spending months at a time alone in a hearing environment without deaf people is unimaginable. I wonder how I would be able to stand it. Would I start screaming again like a seagull? Would I get all worked up? Would I beg them to look at me and not forget I exist?

It's always a relief to get back into a deaf environment. You don't have to wear yourself out using your voice. It's so wonderful to discover your hands again, your spontaneity, signs that fly in the air, that express ideas so effortlessly, so freely. Your body moves. Your eyes speak. Your frustration vanishes in an instant.

It's as smooth as silk.

Chapter 17

Poison Love

I had been told. My father had warned me, "Leave him. He's no good. He'll hurt you."

So had my friends: "He won't be faithful."

And so had my mother: "He's violent."

But I thought, "They don't understand him. He's a misfit because he had problems during his childhood. Maybe he likes to chase after girls, but I'm the one he loves. He's violent, but I'll tame him."

I told myself all kinds of things about him. I arranged them in my mind and wrapped them in the fabric of my trust in him. My trust was absolute. Blind faith. And when I give my trust to that extent, it had better not be taken lightly.

Above all, I was in love. I was drawn to him as if by a magnet and wasn't thinking rationally. My imagination, my ability to see things clearly, had been completely blotted out by my attraction to him. He was as thirsty for love as I was, and we drank of it together.

One day, there was a party at the house. We loved parties. We put the music up full blast and glued our ears to the speakers. We used to hold up the record jackets to let everybody know whether it was rock music or a slow dance. Dancing was a way of releasing tension. You could feel the beat in your feet, in your whole body, and let yourself be pulled along by the physical impulses it sparked. Dancing with HIM.

"Someone told me you were seeing somebody else . . ."

"That's not true. You're the only one. You're my one and only."

Even so, as he was signing, he seemed a bit on the defensive. He stepped back and his signs were somewhat halting. His answer was long and drawn out. He was probably wondering, "What am I going to tell her?"

I guess when a deaf lover lies, it's just as obvious as when a hearing one does. What can probably be deduced from vocal intonation and the indecisiveness of the message can likewise be gathered from the signs, body position, and way a person looks at you.

Personally, I'm not good at lying. I tried it with my parents and it didn't work. This seagull is too honest.

And she's also too naive. I had believed him for so long I needed to see his lies with my own eyes to be convinced.

It had been an hour since I had last seen him and I didn't know where he was. I looked for him all over the house. The only place I hadn't checked was the bathroom. That's where he was, and I had a hunch he wasn't alone.

I decided to spy on him from my bedroom through the transom. I could see everything from there, like a seagull atop the mast of a sailing ship.

This time, his cheating was blatant. I pounded really hard on the bathroom door. He opened it with a big smile and tried to hide the other person. He was trying to cover up the truth, still trying to make me believe he loved me. That was something I couldn't tolerate. I always look at reality head on. I don't hide behind anyone.

I could feel my hatred growing. Pain pierced my heart and a tightness gripped my throat. There are times when you wish you could shout the signs that express all those emotions.

I ran out of the house in a state of mental and emotional confusion, leaving my friends to their partying. They were oblivious to what was going on. I ran so far I didn't know where I was any more.

I took shelter in the entry hall of a building and cried for a long time. Alone, till dawn.

Then the calm returned after the storm of tears that had shaken me. I placidly started walking back home. The sea was calm and the seagull was quietly coming back to port.

He was waiting for me. All upset and feeling guilty because I had disappeared. He looked pathetic. He wanted to say he was sorry, kiss, and make up.

But it was over. I didn't love him any more. Had I ever really loved him or was I only in love with the image I had created of him? And what does faithfulness mean? Or trust?

I was barely seventeen but I had loved him a long time. I was so young when I fell for him. Now I was ready to accept defeat and feel the knife in my heart. But I didn't want it to end there. Since he wanted to play the victim and try to get me to forgive him for his so-called momentary fling, I decided to wait it out patiently and let him taste the poison of treachery, too. I didn't walk out on him right away. I wanted him to feel the same knife wound in his heart.

Hate must be a part of love. Wanting revenge meant I wanted to end the love story. My own story (not just his) brought to a close because of *my* scheming, *my* lies, *my* deceitfulness. That's what I wanted to give him as a good-bye present.

I got the chance soon enough. And it was only after the fact that I made him listen to me tell him point-blank, "There you have it. It's over. I don't love you any more."

My perverted little game of lies and torture no doubt bothered me more than it did him. I don't know if he understood or even noticed anything. He refused to believe I didn't love him any more. He had me say it again. He wanted me to look him straight in the eye.

I was cold, determined not to let that difficult moment drag on forever. He pulled a razor blade out of his pocket.

"Either you stay with me or I'll slash my wrists."

He was subjecting me to the usual blackmail. He wanted *his* death on *my* conscience. I didn't even think twice. I said, "It's over."

And he actually did it! He slit his wrist open in front of me without flinching.

I was horrified and got out of there fast. All that violence! All that blood! He was going to die! It was my fault. He was going to die!

I ran to some friends' house and sobbed over him and over what might happen to me. I could already imagine myself being charged by the police, then going to court, and being sentenced to I didn't know what. Eternal remorse at the very least. I couldn't live with a burden like that on my conscience. I was sure he was dead because I had seen the blood flowing from his veins with my own eyes before I ran out and left him there. I always believed what I saw.

Poor naive little seagull. After a good bandaging job at the hospital, he was fine. Maybe he hadn't realized committing suicide that way wasn't so easy. And neither had I.

Mother consoled and reassured me. She made me stop feeling guilty. Even if the worst had happened, I wasn't to blame. He was the liar. He was the one responsible for the blackmail and for what he had done to himself. I wasn't. You can't be both the guilty party and the victim. People are responsible for their own actions.

As strange as it may seem, any real love I felt for that guy disappeared once and for all the day my parents separated. Once my father was gone from the house, my relationship with the boy I loved died.

After the divorce, the image I had of my father, the male symbol of my childhood, completely vanished.

Communication between my father and me was temporarily severed. Our love was on hold.

And the image I had of my lover when I was thirteen vanished, too. Communication between him and me was cut off forever. Our love was dead.

After that, I distrusted boys for what seemed to be a long time. I became hard and bitter.

I came to realize that there was no such thing as faithfulness and the word *trust* didn't have the same meaning any more.

I roamed around aimlessly for a while in search of other kinds of trust and different poisons. I got high on music and alcohol, frivolous partying, and tobacco. To the point of exhaustion.

Mouette was caught in a net. Polluted.

Chapter 18
Brainless Mouette

It seemed like only yesterday I thought I was happy. I danced and joked and laughed. I stayed out as late as I could. There were no more boys in my life. There was no lover to party with. I went out with the girls to avoid being tricked by lies.

One night, I didn't get back to my father's till dawn. I was staying with him that weekend.

As usual, before I went out, he had told me, "Be careful. Watch out. Don't get back too late. You need your sleep," etc. And I thought to myself, "There he goes again."

Something happened that night. I can't remember what it was very well because of all the alcohol. Everything was spinning around. I didn't know where I was. This time I had gone too far.

Waking up was ugly. Actually, I had been feeling ugly for some time. When I looked in the mirror, I noticed big circles under my eyes. My complexion was gray. I looked awful. I thought, "Why do you look so bad? You've got to stop drinking, kiddo. There's nothing going on in your head. All you do is party and drink. Just look at yourself!"

Mouette looked pretty bad off. Mouette decided she was a stupid jerk. But then she would do it all over again the next day.

At home, I quarreled with my sister. Marie had grown up. The last time we argued was over something stupid. She never put her things away. They were lying all over the room, and we shared the same closet.

"Put your things away. Don't throw your clothes everywhere."

"Leave me alone."

"If you don't put your things away, I'll get really mad and won't talk to you any more."

"It's not my fault that the closet's in your room!"

"Exactly! You're in *my* room. Put your stuff away!"

"Quit bugging me. I've got work to do."

I physically pulled her into the room to make her put her things away. She was screaming. I couldn't control myself. We loved each other but we squabbled just the same. This time she didn't think it was funny when I said, "You're a little tchit!"

"Shit" is "tifikul" to pronounce. It's like the *s* in "talami." I have trouble with *s* and *sh* sounds. No big deal.

At the time, the only messiness I was guilty of was in my head. The only place things were messed-up was under my hair. On the outside, I was always straightening things up, the way I used to arrange my dolls when I was little.

It was true that Marie had grown. Before, she would have gone running to my mother to tell on me. We would have pulled each other's hair and I would have gotten yelled at. Now she sulked and didn't say anything to Mother. She could stand on her own two feet, like a big person. And when she sulked, she wouldn't sign to me at all.

She had started correcting my mistakes in French, too. She was at the head of her class in everything. My little sister Marie was catching up with me and the ten years of independence I'd had.

Everything was a mess!

One night, I collapsed in the hall. It woke up my father and stepmother. He had to pick me up and carry me to bed. I was sick . . . sicker than I had ever been before.

He was sitting at my bedside in the morning light. His face frightened me. I was ashamed that he could see what a wreck I was, what a state I was in. I was ashamed, and really bad off both mentally and physically. I said, "I had a lot to drink yesterday."

"I know. No need to explain. I can see that."

He was worried.

"Alcohol is supposed to make you happy, and make dancing and partying more fun. Everyone I hang out with drinks."

I tried to tell my father it wasn't serious.

"It's dangerous. Very dangerous. Bad for the brain. It kills brain cells, you know. Look at me, Emmanuelle. Why are you doing it? I don't understand."

Neither did I. I thought it was to have a good time. It made me high. It was like flying. It made me forget. But forget what? I had even forgotten what I wanted to forget. It was impossible to explain to him how bad I felt about myself. Maybe I wanted him to take care of me. We saw so little of each other. Maybe I was trying to provoke him because I needed him. Why was I drinking, chain-smoking, dancing all night, and raising hell till dawn only to collapse in a stupor and wake up looking like I did? I have no idea.

"You have to tell my why, Emmanuelle."

My father is very philosophical and theoretical. A real psychiatrist and a real father, surprised at the child he had produced. Perplexed by his seagull's flight. Bewildered. He really wanted answers to his questions. Answers like, "I'm scared of the world. I don't like life." And maybe, "I'm deaf. I've got problems."

After we got back from Washington, he had decided to work with the deaf. He always said there was no such thing as "deaf psychology." Just deaf people. And each one is unique, as is the case with hearing people. The only difference is that deaf people have their own language. Many believe the deaf are incapable of establishing contacts and having normal relationships with people. My father fought against that view. The deaf are like the hearing. There are mentally ill people among the deaf the way there are among the hearing population. It's not something specific to us. Deaf people are doing quite well, thank you. But in spite of it all, my father may have been concerned that my behavior at the time was related to my deafness. Maybe I was having trouble adapting, and that was why I was using alcohol as an escape and doing stupid things. I don't think so. That wasn't it, Dad.

I wasn't alone. Adolescence is tough for some kids, deaf or not. Some navigate easily between the ages of thirteen and eighteen. Others make a wrong turn. Some forge headlong into the storm like me, but they never come back. Others end up grabbing onto a lifesaver to keep from sinking. It depends on so many parameters. Education, temperament, love, environment. Adolescence creates a complicated sort of alchemy. When you're a teenager, you hunt for the philosopher's stone as if it actually existed.

My father asked me every question imaginable. What areas was I having problems in? Where was I feeling frustrated? Was it at school? Was I in love? Why was I drinking? Why was I doing this or that? Why everything?

And I had only one answer for his avalanche of questions, "I don't feel good about myself. I need you."

There was a deathly silence. An uncomfortable, pensive moment filled with emotion and consternation. I could instinctively sense all those things in him just by looking. But it wasn't a solution.

"Tomorrow, I'm taking you to the doctor. I want to see if you're in good health."

"Okay."

Okay for going to the doctor's. But it still wasn't a solution. My father couldn't take care of me. He didn't know how. Or he didn't want to. That's what I believed at the time. It hurt. It was a new wound that would take a long time to heal.

Mouette, you're a problem child. You still need to grow up. Without your dad. You need to accept your parents' separation, come to terms with it, and make your nest on another rock.

That's what I told myself later. But at seventeen, you just feel bad. There's no way you can feel good about yourself. You think you're ugly and worthless.

Brainless.

I went to see the doctor with Dad. By the way, I don't know if there are any deaf doctors in France. When I go to the doctor's, I can get by with reading lips and writing out what I want to tell him. But if he starts using technical words or talking about medication, I'm totally lost.

Dad listened to what the doctor had to say, then interpreted for me. It came as no surprise. There was nothing good about the mess I was in. I wanted to feel good about myself and now I felt even worse. Really awful. Physically and psychologically. Physically, I felt like a limp rag. I even had bruises everywhere from falling when I was drunk. Psychologically, I felt completely worthless.

I had wanted to go beyond my limits and I had done just that. I didn't want to face reality. Okay, I had succeeded in avoiding it. I wanted to run away from my deaf problems, from school, from my social life. As a result, what had I learned between the ages of sixteen and seventeen?

That last night of carousing was a turning point. All of a sudden, I thought, "I've had it. That's it. I can't go on like this any more. I haven't done anything with my life. I'm useless. Where am I headed? All I do is hang out with the gang, griping and protesting. We feel oppressed. We get pissed off. We party. Cool. Cool? Actually, when you get right down to it, nothing ever really happens. It's always the same old thing. We always go to the same old place together. It's always the same old faces. Nothing ever changes. What's constructive about that? What do you get out of drowning yourself in a bottle of whisky? You're totally disoriented, like a drunk bird that has lost its bearings.

"Mouette, you're really brainless. You need to ease up and start feeling good. You need to get pleasure out of something besides partying. You need to be independent, get a job and earn some money. Vacation is coming. It'll be the first time you leave home alone. Get yourself back on your feet again!"

Chapter 19

All the Suns of the World

I started thinking about the future—something I hadn't done in a long time.

When I first learned sign language at age seven, I had lots of questions about what I would do with my life. Would I have a job? What would it be? What could I learn to do? It seemed that those same concerns were resurfacing. The same refreshing waves of desire, discovery, and curiosity about the future were washing back over me. The parenthetical gap of my teen years, my turbulent "anything goes" phase, was over.

I talked about my prospects with my mother. What path should I follow? Which road should I take? Did I want to work with the deaf? See only deaf people? Go to college? If I did, I could teach others and promote bilingual education after I finished.

But I had always loved the creative arts. Where can you learn things like that when you're deaf?

Maybe I didn't have to go to college. I could learn about life in other ways and in other places. Like the theater. I had always wanted to be an actress. It's an idea that came to me almost by chance, after I had done a two-week theater training program when I was around eight or nine. I performed with three other deaf children on Wednesdays and Saturdays. Ralph Robbins was in charge of it. He had come from New York to work with the IVT (International Visual Theater). He had us use masks we had made ourselves and work on body expression. That was important because, as children, we had a tendency to mostly observe faces. To get us out of that habit, Ralph had us wear expressionless neutral white masks. I realized what he wanted—for us to rely on our bodies to express ourselves. It was hard, but fascinating. I was excited about being able to use my body along with my hands and face to communicate.

My theatrical career started, thanks to Ralph, with a short play called *Journey to the End of the Metro*. It was the story of a little girl who falls asleep while riding the metro and forgets to get off at her stop. She gets lost in the underground passageways at the end of the line where she meets a magician with four arms. The story was more or less about me because, every Saturday, I used to take the bus, train, and metro to get to Vincennes. It took an hour and a half. That was long and tiring for a little nine-year-old, and I often fell asleep. Based on that, we wrote the rest of the story with Ralph.

I was sad when Ralph left to go back home. I didn't get over it for a long time. I really liked him. He was tall, gentle, imaginative, and enthusiastic. He taught us a lot. I especially liked how he coached us onstage.

I just loved the theater. It was a ray of sunlight in my childhood. I owe my name sign to the theater: "Sun-Coming-from-the-Heart." It's a line from a poem that deaf actress Chantal Liennel had written: "Thanks Dad, thanks Mom, for giving me the sun coming from the heart."

Alfredo Corrado only worked with adults at the theater in Vincennes. "Finish school," he used to tell me, "then we'll see what you can do."

I had a bit part on TV once. They filmed it at the *foire du Trône* (a fair held annually in Vincennes). I was nine and it was sheer heaven. There were white circus dogs on the set. I was supposed to comb a mermaid's long, flowing hair and tell her she was beautiful. But the mermaid didn't like having her hair combed so they had to keep redoing the scene! On the tenth take, she broke down and went to her dressing room, sobbing. I was so afraid she would quit and I'd lose my bit part in that movie magic. When she came back on the set, I gave her a hug. The eleventh take went right, and was I ever glad!

I love films. I think I've seen every movie Charlie Chaplin ever made. Chaplin is my point of reference because of the laughs and emotion he can get out of audiences. He's proof that words aren't indispensable when you know how to speak with your body. Genius isn't necessarily based on sentences. Chaplin was a prophet, and *The Great Dictator* is a marvelous testimony to that. The main character plays with a balloon that represents the world. He throws it, spins it like a top, catches it, and turns it till it finally explodes in his face! Chaplin could reach all kinds of audiences, all sorts of people. I dream that someday there'll be another Chaplin and that I'll make the plunge into movies. Why not?

With the exception of subtitled American films, movies in France are for hearing people. Did I really want to be assimilated into the hearing world? Did I want to see new things?

Yes. First of all, I wanted to see the world. I wanted to open myself up to it more and overcome my fears. There. I've admitted it. I was a little afraid of the hearing world. It was time for me to grapple with it.

"Finish school first!" Mom and Dad said. "If you drop out, what will you do? Finish school first!"

This time, my reaction wasn't, "There they go again." I didn't know what I was going to do afterwards, but I would finish school first.

Mouette, you're not as brainless as you thought.

It took me three more years in the Morvan program to get ready for the baccalaureate exam: the seventeenth, eighteenth, and nineteenth years of my life. I made up my mind when I was seventeen that I was going to study hard. I would get my diploma if it killed me. I was going to take school seriously when I went back in the fall. The freedom I had been clamoring for had to start with me. It couldn't come from anywhere else.

But first, there was summer and sun. I needed to build my health back up. I did a few odd jobs—babysitting, like all teenage girls. Taking care of little kids was good for me. It took me back to my childhood, when my mother used to say, "Don't slam doors! Just because you're deaf doesn't mean you have to make noise."

And deaf children do make noise. When I was babysitting, I was mindful of the neighbors downstairs. Just like my mother, I would say, "Don't stamp your feet. Don't bounce the ball on the wall. Don't jump like that."

I remember my first babysitting job. Two sisters. One was deaf and the other hearing, like Marie and me. But in their case, it was the older girl who could hear. She was nine and her sister, six. We used sign language to talk to each other.

Their way of expressing themselves was really cute. Their little hands danced in the air. It was childlike, different from adult language. They were just adorable and both as lovable as could be. Their signs were very precise. More so perhaps than words spoken by hearing children.

I thought of myself at their age. They were lucky to be able to sign so proficiently, so beautifully at such an early age, unlike myself. I got a late start. They had active minds and asked loads of questions.

"Is it bad to be deaf?"

"Of course not."

"Why do doctors say they have to take care of us? Does that mean we're going to die?"

"Of course not! I'll tell you all about it."

We looked at *Tintin* comics, too, and I signed the words and dialogs that appeared in the balloons for them. I acted out the *Tintin in Tibet* story and pretended to be Captain Haddock.

For my second job, I had to babysit two boys, ages four and seven. Boys are more of a problem. They never stop running around. The little one was a terror, and I had a lot of trouble trying to get him to slow down. Plus they really made a racket. It didn't bother me if they screamed and slammed doors. But I was more concerned about the people downstairs.

"Stop it! You're not the only ones living here!"

I was obviously growing up because I was talking like my mother. But the boys couldn't have cared less.

"So what! We're deaf!"

"Yes, but other people can hear!"

"I'd rather live in a building just for deaf people. That way, they'd leave us alone!"

I had to laugh. Finally I could laugh whenever something struck me as clever, true, or witty. I took pleasure in small things, like the smile on other people's faces, the restful summer ahead of me, or just thinking about my future.

Taking care of those door-slamming rascals allowed me to put some money aside for my vacation.

I worked part-time at my grandfather's lab. Henri Laborit, my paternal grandfather, is an amazing man. I call him Grandfather Lab. I didn't know a lot about him because he worked so much that we rarely saw each other. At one point in his research, he became fascinated by a molecule whose name I can't pronounce for the life of me (chlorpromazine!). Thanks to him, that little molecule became pretty important. It served as the basis for the world's first tranquilizer, and has since given rise to several others.

My grandfather explores and researches the biological world. Over the years, he has gone from molecule to molecule, working on new drugs for anesthesia, cardiology, psychiatry, etc. He has studied human behavior and written tons of books. I was told that when he was little, he used to catch grasshoppers and put them in a shoe box to study them. I think he was five at the time. A child prodigy.

He started out as a marine surgeon (the Laborit family loves the sea), but eventually ended up in biological research. He has so many important accomplishments to his credit! He even had an impact on the movie industry! The French director, Alain Resnais, based his film *My Uncle from America* on my grandfather's most famous book, *Decoding the Human Message*. Grandfather is quite a scholar.

He's quite a sailor, too. Once, when I was little, he took me out on his boat. Fond memories of the sun and sea.

Grandfather Lab often did experiments with rats. His laboratory was kind of a weird place. I was in charge of keeping it clean: washing off the tiled tables he used for his experiments, sweeping out the rat droppings, rinsing out the test-tubes and putting them in the sterilizer. One or two hours a day, every day but Sunday, I would plug away at bringing order to the slight disorder of my grandfather's great research. He was a scientific wizard.

I earned more money for my vacation. July seemed endless in Paris, but the August sun on the Spanish island of Ibiza was waiting for me.

The beach. The ocean. The sun. I really love the sun. The sun everywhere, in every country: Morocco, Spain, Greece, Italy. One day, I'll see all the suns of the world.

The water and sun on my body all day long. The innocent, sensual pleasure of the waves. Each day on Ibiza was a celebration of light, and each night was gentle and breezy in my hair, fragrant and shimmering on my golden skin.

I was starting to like myself a little more. I ran into some deaf people on the island quite by chance. They were from Italy and Spain. We made small talk and I got to know their "accent," that is, their particular signs. And they learned mine.

There I was with my best friend, totally free. Ibiza was marvelous. We talked about everything. I started reading again, and read a lot. There were other pleasures, too. First and foremost was freedom: having a wallet, a budget, money she and I had earned, watching our expenses. We weren't accountable to anyone except ourselves, regardless of how we spent our money.

I was feeling a lot better. I was happy. I felt like a free, responsible individual with no authority figure around to tell me what to do. I was my own person. And I had stopped doing stupid things.

My mother called. She had somehow been able to reach me there on my sun-drenched island to tell me about another kind of sun. Ariane Mnouchkine was making a film and needed extras.

I had to take a boat and train right away to be on location: the National Assembly in Paris. I was so afraid of not having enough money for my trip back that I asked my mother to send me some. As it turned out, I realized I didn't need it. I had successfully managed my very first budget all by myself!

Ariane selected extras for her film from actors who were in the *Théâtre du Soleil* (Sun Theater) company. There were Chinese, Indians, Blacks, Jews, Arabs, handicapped people, blind people, dwarfs, and deaf people. The planet Earth in miniature. It was a kaleidoscope, a bouquet of different flowers. They were all there in the film to witness the reading of the declaration of human rights. That was the scene I was in. I was one of all those flowers that life had brought together in the sunlight of the cameras.

My scene lasted thirty seconds. I was part of a group of deaf people watching an interpreter translate as someone read the declaration of human rights. Then we all said, "Fantastic. We're all equal. We finally have our rights."

Ariane Mnouchkine was amazingly authoritative and precise. She was efficient, decisive, and sensitive, and kept an eye on every detail. In sign language, we called her "Woman-with-Her-Arms-on-Her-Legs."

I met Simon, an Armenian, who was one of the actors in the film. He had no trouble communicating with the deaf even though he didn't use speech or sign language. He had an extraordinary talent for speaking with his hands and an unusual gift for externalizing.

He and everyone else motivated me to go on and pursue the idea of working in the theater.

After that, I was in the *fête du Regard,* a visual festival bringing together the hearing and deaf for short, five-minute skits. One of the festival themes was Black and White, so I asked my uncle to write something about day and night that my childhood friend, Claire, and I could act out. I was Night and she was Day. We translated the dialog into sign language and added a little improvisation.

CLAIRE (as DAY): Good day, Ma'am!

EMMANUELLE (as NIGHT): Why "good day"? You know very well that I'm Night! Mr. Day! You're making fun of me!

In another skit, Claire and I played the part of two hands. Claire was one and I was the other. The hands fought. We acted out the quarrel, then the separation, and reconciliation. Working hands and idle hands. Hands that dominate and hands that are dominated.

We could do whatever we wanted for the next theme, so a bunch of us teenagers appeared dressed in white under an ultraviolet light. The story was very visual. A child falls asleep at school and has a dream. There were special effects. It looked like his head was separating from his body and his arms and legs were coming off as the dream turned into a restless nightmare. His head seemed to be floating off on its own while the headless body went in another direction. It was beautiful and the audience applauded. I could really feel it. I could see it. I could feel the vibrations, the intensity. Every audience has its own particular rhythm.

I love the theater. I love the stage and the applause. But . . . finish school first.

Chapter 20

AIDS and the Sun

Like so many, they die because of lack of information. In my "wild and crazy youth," I had never even thought about it. But I could have stumbled on someone who was HIV-positive and contracted AIDS without knowing it. Fortunately, in the gang I partied with, we smoked joints once in a while, but never shot up on heroine. No syringes. Even so, we weren't up on things and, at the time, couldn't have cared less. I didn't get clued in till I was seventeen.

Information campaigns on AIDS are organized by hearing people for hearing people. The ads they run on TV aren't captioned and neither are televised medical programs. I don't care if variety shows aren't captioned, but I'm appalled that television is more concerned about ratings than about the information it dispenses (which should be its primary responsibility). AIDS kills deaf people because they don't have enough information about it. I consider withholding information like that a criminal offense.

Everything and everyone contributes to this tragic situation: doctors who can't sign, parents who don't teach their children about AIDS, newspapers that the deaf rarely read, hospitals where the only concern is to inform the hearing.

It even includes the logo used to represent the HIV virus. A hearing person might think it's funny that someone would equate AIDS with the sun. Yet some deaf people, fortunately they're not in the majority, believe that AIDS is transmitted by the sun. That's because the HIV virus is often represented by a small orange circle with spikes coming out of it. The symbol could easily be taken for the sun. It's those orange spikes the hearing people behind the campaign found so eye-catching that have given rise to the confusion.

AIDS = sun = danger! The only precautionary measure deaf people convinced of that logic take is staying out of the sun! They shun the symbol of life because they're afraid it might kill them.

Here's another example of misinformation I know about. A doctor told his deaf patient that his test was HIV-positive. To reassure him, the doctor told him that being HIV-positive didn't mean he had AIDS, so he didn't need to take safety measures right away. To the deaf patient, that implied he wasn't sick and therefore didn't need to be on medication. He could lead a normal life. So there you have a deaf person who walked out of the doctor's office with a completely erroneous notion in his head and who probably unwittingly spread the virus. The mistake is unforgivable.

Bruno Moncelle, a friend of mine, asked me to join a volunteer group formed in 1989 as part of the French organization called AIDES. I went through a training session along with other deaf friends to learn more about the disease and to think of ways to better disseminate information to the deaf community.

It wasn't enough to merely provide emotional support to AIDS victims. Prevention was critical. We urgently needed to find a code in sign language that would make it clear to everyone how the disease was transmitted, and organize meetings in educational centers to explain it.

During the information sessions I participated in with Bruno Moncelle, I heard some astounding answers to his question, "Can anyone here tell me how you get AIDS?"

Answers:

"By kissing?"

"When you have spots on your face."

"When you have pimples."

"You shouldn't kiss."

"I don't know."

"AIDS isn't a problem for me. I don't have it."

Bruno tried to explain that you have to be very careful because there aren't any visual warning signs. If a person is losing weight, it might be because he or she isn't eating. Blotches on someone's face might be the result of having been out in the sun. There's no way of seeing AIDS. For deaf people, the total absence of visual markers is a kind of blindness, a wall between them and understanding. It was crucial to impress upon them the virus's insidious, dormant nature. The absence of visible symptoms.

Bruno explained that the disease erupts later, after the body has been infected with the virus. It remains dormant for a long time and then one day becomes active. He used an egg as an example. You don't see what's inside the egg. But there's a baby chick sleeping in there. The hen sits on the egg and one day the chick comes out.

But the virus isn't a cute little chick. It's a vampire that eats away at the body from inside.

Something that had a big impact on young people was the case of the great American basketball player, Magic Johnson, who was courageous enough to come out publicly and admit he was HIV-positive. His message came across, especially to deaf boys who watch a lot of sports on television. One of the boys at a session had seen Johnson when he was in peak form and asked if he wouldn't be able to play any more.

I used Bruno's analogy to explain to him that the virus was dormant, like a baby chick in an egg. Johnson wasn't sick, but one day when the monster chick came out, it would invade his entire body and that would be the end for him. He wouldn't be able to play. He'd be very sick.

Then Bruno handed out condoms and gave some very straight-forward advice: Wear a condom when you have sex and you won't get AIDS. Don't wear one and you'll get it.

The AIDES deaf chapter invented a special sign to symbolize the virus. You take your right hand and make a circle by rounding your thumb and index finger, keeping your other fingers straight and spread apart to make spikes while cupping your left hand underneath. We also made a video which, at the time of this writing, has yet to be distributed and shown!

This is a battle that I think is extremely important for our community. I help out with distributing information on AIDS every time I'm asked, and I've been doing it ever since I was seventeen. We still have work to do in the area of making people understand the various ways the virus is transmitted. But what we're asking the government to do is go into the schools, form groups, and organize lectures for the deaf. Bruno Moncelle's courage, intelligence, and dedication deserve not only to be encouraged but aided as well.

Let me say it again: There are three and a half million deaf people in France who can vote, just like everybody else, but who also make love and have children, just like everybody else. And it's their right to be informed, just like everybody else.

AIDS SUN: much too pretty to symbolize a killer vampire in the night.

Chapter 21

It Gets Me So Aggravated!

Deaf education in France stops with the baccalaureate exam. In the Morvan program, preparatory work for the exam takes three years. A few deaf students go on to college. One of my deaf friends did, but it's extremely hard. Like doing ten times the work. She photocopied notes from a hearing student in the class. If she didn't know anybody in class, she had to make other arrangements. One of her friends turned note-taking into a regular job and now acts as a relay for deaf students.

As soon as she got home, she would start studying. But because she was using someone else's notes, she had absolutely no way of hooking into things that person may have heard but not bothered to jot down. Besides, unlike hearing students, she couldn't ask the teacher to clarify specific points after class. If she didn't get something, she just had to manage as best she could. A lot of time was wasted.

Another method my friend used was to tape the lectures. Then her mother or father, who were both hearing, would write them out. It took inordinate amounts of time before she could get down and really study. One day she told me, "It's hell. It's so ridiculous. Everything's double work. A few of my friends finally got their general studies diploma (*DEUG*) or other university degrees, but they're the exceptions."

My friend is profoundly deaf, like me. She hadn't been signing that long and her parents never learned. So she couldn't use sign language to get help from them.

Even so, she passed her baccalaureate exam, then took preparatory courses in biology and special math. In college, she had to take her first-year courses twice. The last I heard, she was getting ready to start her third year.

Deaf people always have to take courses a second time. It's inevitable since they only get fifty percent of the course material from lipreading. It gets me so aggravated!

I had a friend who left the Morvan program because her parents moved away from Paris. I remember when we were in class together, she used to say to me, "Your mother signs. That's terrific. It's really incredible."

She wanted so much for her parents to learn sign language. When I was invited to her house, we would have dinner with her family. Obviously, I wasn't going to sit there all evening without saying anything, so the first time I was there, I started signing. Her parents stopped me right away.

"Don't do that. You have to use your voice."

"But I'm talking to her. I'm not going to voice to a deaf person!"

It would have been so artificial and stupid! Using my voice with them was one thing, since they didn't know my language. But with my friend?

"I'm sorry, but I think it's ridiculous to voice with her!"

"Use your voice, otherwise we can't understand what you're saying!"

Not only did they prevent her from expressing herself naturally with me, but on top of it, they wanted to know everything we were saying to each other! So what happens to individual freedom in a situation like that?

My friend rebelled against her parents. Later, she told me her relationship with them was horrible and that they used to have terrible fights. Her father was violent by nature, so there was always hostility and conflict in the air at their house. Sometimes she would explode and knock over furniture because she needed a physical outlet for all the tension inside her. I was astounded by their behavior. I couldn't imagine a relationship like that with my mother or father.

When I couldn't stomach going to her house any more, she started coming to mine. We could talk freely there. Nevertheless, she made it a point to use her voice with my mother, even though my mother knew LSF.

We could relax and talk for hours in my room. She told me the story of her life and I told her mine. It helped her cope with her situation.

Her parents had a negative image of her. They considered her handicapped, sick. In their view, their daughter would never be "normal" unless they hid her deafness and made her use her voice. Like so many people, they thought that if she used sign, she would never speak. That really has nothing to do with it. When I was seven, I could talk but I used to say anything that popped into my head. Then, because of sign language, I began to speak much better. Oral French wasn't my only option any more, so psychologically I could accept it much easier. What's more, sign language helped me process important information—concepts and thoughts. Writing became easier and so did reading. I benefited so much from it that, to my mind, it would be totally unfair to deprive any deaf child of sign language. It shouldn't be assumed that a child has to be able to speak to know how to read and write. When I read a novel, I instinctively associate the corresponding sign with the word I'm reading. Then I can read the word more easily on people's lips when they pronounce it. My visual memory even jibes perfectly with French spelling. A word is an image or symbol. When I was taught *yesterday* and *tomorrow* in sign language, when I understood their meaning, I was able to say the words more easily and it was easier to write them, too!

In my mind, a written word has the face of a word the way a clown has the face of a clown. Mother has the face of Mother, my sister the face of my sister! I can recognize a word's face! And draw it in the air. And write it! And say it! And be bilingual.

I wouldn't have wanted to trade places with my friend. Her parents' love for her was self-centered. They wanted her to be like them. Mine accepted incredibly well the fact that I was different, and they shared my difference with me. She, on the other hand, couldn't share anything important with her mother. How could she tell her what she felt deep inside, all her problems as a child and then as a teenager, her love life, disappointments, and joys? All that was important to her. It gets me so aggravated!

Communication between my friend and her parents remained superficial, limited to the words she spoke. It was perfectly normal under the circumstances that she didn't get along with them. They knew nothing about her. Or almost nothing. And she didn't know anything about them. She was so alone!

But I know of an even worse case: the astounding story of a girl named Sylvie who lived in a family environment that I have trouble believing could even exist. Until the age of fifteen, Sylvie was convinced she was the only deaf person in the world—**the only one.** It wasn't just something she imagined, but a reality for her. Her parents had told her point-blank that she was the only living deaf specimen. She was an oddity, a freak—and why not go all the way?—circus material. And so she grew up in ignorance, in the loneliness of what she believed was her unparalleled difference, desperately trying to talk like Mommy and Daddy, and her hearing classmates. She bore her "curse" all alone.

When I was little and they told me I was deaf, I imagined that my auditory nerve was all shriveled up. That's how I saw it, in images. But my parents corrected me right away.

"Of course not," they said. "The nerve isn't shriveled up. It's there. It's just like ours, only it doesn't work."

That's the impression I've had of my deafness ever since: My nerve doesn't work. It's a straightforward explanation and it's accurate, too. Thanks, Mom and Dad.

But what about Sylvie? She didn't even have a mental image to cling to. Nothing. Because they didn't tell her the truth.

But the truth always comes out eventually. One day, a classmate of hers betrayed the family secret. He let Sylvie know that there were actually other deaf people in the world, and that he had met some personally in the metro. Sylvie didn't believe him. There was no way she could ever question the sacred word of her all-powerful procreators. Her devotion to them was unwavering. Naturally, as the "only abnormal person in the world," she felt both guilty and blessed for existing because of them. But she was tormented by what her friend had told her. She had to know for sure. She had to erase all doubt. So she made a bet with her hearing friend and went to check it out with him, convinced that her parents were right.

One Friday after school, the two of them went to the metro. The station is literally swarming with young deaf people on Friday nights. There's always a mixture of different nationalities, and everybody's talking and gesturing energetically.

Sylvie looked at the throng practically blocking the entire station. What were they doing? What were all those gestures? What did it mean? She finally realized they were deaf. All of them. Men, women, teenagers—all deaf. The shock was so great she started vomiting. She was shaken to the very depths of her being. Her world had been turned upside down. Dozens, hundreds of deaf people? She couldn't accept that. She was incapable of coming to terms with what she had discovered at the age of fifteen.

When she got home, she let her parents have it. They became the victims of their own wrongful, inexcusable silence. Sylvie flew into a rage. She felt anger, humiliation, wrath. How could her own parents have denied her identity to such an extent? Their answer: "It was for your own good."

To Sylvie's parents I say, "You did it to segregate your daughter from her own kind. So the neighbors wouldn't know. So your daughter would use her voice. So she'd be more like you, not like herself. Especially so she wouldn't be herself!"

Sylvie demanded that her parents transfer her to a school where she could meet deaf students. She courageously began to learn sign language, slowly but surely. With great difficulty but also with great determination, she was able to integrate a world that nonetheless continued to marginalize her on one side or the other. Then, over the course of time, her behavior changed. Sign language allowed her to blossom and be happy. She told me she has forgiven her parents now. I love Sylvie for her courage and for what she went through and overcame. Fifteen years of lies! It gets me so aggravated!

It's the same thing with politics. Except for some of the president's speeches, televised political addresses are never captioned. Yet there are three and a half million of us deaf people in France and, as far as I know, we still have the right to vote! True, there are newspapers, but what a politician says at a particular moment, the expressions he makes, his way of saying it, the words he uses, that all counts, too.

One day I was surprised by some racist comments at a deaf bikers' club! The only politician they could understand by reading lips was a person whose name I don't have the slightest desire to mention here.

Those young deaf people told me, "We voted for him because he uses simple words that can be lipread easily. He enunciates well. We can't understand the other politicians when they talk."

"France for the French" can easily be lipread! But the racism behind those words, the exclusionary attitude and dangers hearing people can deduce from the speaker's tone were nonexistent for those young deaf people. Has anyone appeared on TV to tell them via captioning, "Here's what that man is saying and, from a humanitarian perspective, it's unacceptable"? After that, it's their decision, but what gets me riled is that right now they don't have a choice!

I'm really scandalized that those guys are basing the way they vote solely on what they're able to read on one man's lips! Or that they don't vote at all because they can't understand anything the other candidates say! I told them, "Once, in the course of history, there was another man who enunciated so well that he screamed every single syllable. He stuck yellow stars on Jews, pink triangles on homosexuals, and blue triangles on the handicapped. That included deaf people. The stars and triangles were exterminated color by color. He sterilized the deaf so they wouldn't have children."

Politicians have to try to do more than just provide the perfunctory captioning of the President's Christmas message. We don't vote at Christmas time! It gets me so aggravated!

Once at a colloquium we met the former cabinet minister for the disabled. He was in a wheelchair himself, and was very nice, but he was totally unaware of what it meant to be deaf. He kept saying, "If you want to fit in with the hearing world, the first thing you need to do is start using your voice."

What did he mean by "fit in"? Where were all the schools we had told him we needed to make headway in both our languages? Where were all the centers for young deaf people? Where were the AIDS information centers for the deaf? Where was anything we had been asking for?

All he could do was repeat, "Speak and you'll fit in!"

Finally a deaf person, angered by what the ex-minister was saying, stood up and retorted, "If I have to speak, then you get up and walk!"

Was that mean? Of course it was, but it was also a form of black humor. Sometimes that helps.

Politicians annoy me. They're like violins. As I said earlier, I can't feel any vibrations from violins. The notes are too high. Too complicated. Too meandering. Violin music is impossible for me to imagine. I need to have my feet on the ground, so I can feel music that's real.

It gets me so aggravated!

Chapter 22

Quiet . . .
I'm Studying

If I had had a French teacher who could sign like my mother (even with the mistakes she still makes and that make me laugh), I wouldn't have been so afraid of my baccalaureate exam. But I had to lipread. I had to figure out one word from what I saw on those lips, then a second word, until I could finally put one sentence together. In all, I spent ten years in the Morvan program. It's a private school and, although they use the oral method, I'm grateful for the education I got there.

I always had my nose in dictionaries and books, trying to find the exact meaning of sentences I had read on the teacher's lips. I really crammed for my courses. Sometimes I would study like mad until two or three in the morning. Being bilingual helped me tremendously. Spelling wasn't a problem. It was easy for me to remember my mistakes because I visualized them. But sentences with conjunctions like *although* and *while* were complicated. The grammar isn't the same in sign language. And I always wanted to have good sentence structure and a nice style in French. I wanted my style to be scholarly. Perfect.

My sister was way ahead of me on that one. I had taught her how to sign flawlessly and was proud of it. Now, it was her turn to correct my French compositions.

"What's this *because* doing here?" Marie used to say. "Why did you put it there? You have too many *which*'s and *that*'s, and they're not in the right places."

I read stacks of newspapers and studied till I couldn't see straight. My head was so stuffed with facts that I must have looked absolutely dazed half the time.

It's my nature to want to excel, to finish what I start. When I decide to accomplish something, I don't give up. Nothing, or almost nothing, stops me. Stubborn seagull. Obstinate, tired Mouette.

1991. First try at the baccalaureate exam for Emmanuelle Laborit. I was nineteen. Frightened. Scared to death.

I wanted so much to pass. I had worked so hard, day and night. But I was unbelievably nervous and I just went to pieces. I failed.

A failure is hard to take, especially such a stupid one. I had been shot down by fear. Mouette was demoralized. I really felt like giving up.

When you got right down to it, did I really need to pass that exam? What if I just packed it in?

"No. Don't do that," said my parents. "Stick with it. Start over. If you give up, you won't have many options for the future. Go for it!" They were giving me the old "finish school first" line again.

I begged my parents to let me take correspondence courses in addition to my other classes so that I could really get into the finish-school-first mind-set and not get discouraged. That way, I could make up for the fifty percent I wasn't getting at school in geometry, philosophy, history, French, English, biology, etc. At least math uses signs.

I had to start reading and writing as much as possible. I liked history but memorizing facts isn't enough when you have to write an essay on a specific history topic. You need to be able to write flawlessly.

I was one of the rare students in the Morvan program who read a lot. As a general rule, deaf people don't read very much. It's hard for them. They mix up the principles of oral and written expression. They consider written French a language for hearing people. In my opinion, though, reading is more or less image-based. It's visual. But it depends on your training. I was taught to like novels and history. If I don't understand something, I look it up in a dictionary. My parents love to read and write, and it must have rubbed off on me.

Inflation. Deflation. Global economy. Philosophy. The Minitel gets a real workout from students studying for their baccalaureate exam. One student I know actually improved his French dramatically with the Minitel. Before, he was really bad. But the Minitel forced him to write. Now he writes all the time. His grammar is still a little shaky, but his vocabulary is much better.

The prospect of taking the oral part of the exam made me turn blue with fright, as we say in French. I'll add green and black to that!

1992. I would soon be twenty. Last try.

Chapter 23
Silent Glances

I had one more semester to go. That's when, out of the blue, the children of silence came into my life!

I had seen a French production of the play *Children of a Lesser God* (or, as it's called in French, *Les Enfants du silence*—the children of silence) when I was ten at the *Studio des Champs-Élysées* with my parents. The play was originally written by Mark Medoff for a deaf actress friend, Phyllis Frelich. The French female lead was played by Chantal Liennel, the same person who had given me my name sign, "Sun-Coming-from-the-Heart," when I was little.

Since I was only ten when I saw the play, I didn't fully understand it. I remember the general mood of the performance more than anything else—the stage, the characters, a hearing guy, a woman who signed, the conflict between two worlds.

Then one day, my mother said, "Emmanuelle, there's a stage director who wants to see you about a new production of *Children of a Lesser God*. I made an appointment with him for you."

Emotion. Jitters.

The day of our appointment, Jean Dalric showed up wearing a big coat and stylish suit. And there I was, a high schooler in blue jeans and a sweatshirt.

He looked at me. There was something in that look. Hands that spoke my language.

Without hesitating, he said, "Appearance-wise, you're exactly what I had in mind for the role of Sarah! A lot of people have tried to dissuade me from hiring a deaf actress for *Children of a Lesser God,* but I've decided otherwise. It's not fair to exclude the deaf from cultural life and the work place. I think it's really scandalous!"

One day, I asked him why he was so interested in the deaf, why he had committed himself so fully to them, what it was that tied him so strongly to them. There was a moment of silence. Flustered by my question, he thought awhile, then answered, "I don't know. I feel like I'm part of the same family."

Sarah. The female lead!

"Keep in mind that Emmanuelle is an amateur actress," Mother said. "She's never acted professionally. Just for fun. Don't tempt her with a part she might not be able to handle."

Mother was wary of him. Afraid he might try to take her little seagull for a ride. A typical maternal reaction. She was apprehensive of anything that might hurt me. But he wasn't out to do that. And if anyone should have been apprehensive, it was me, Mom. I was a big girl.

Jean asked if we could meet and talk on a regular basis so he could gauge my acting ability. I was skeptical: "You say you want me for the part, but you just might be wrong about me."

"I'm rarely wrong about things."

It's not easy to trust a stranger. But I went with my instincts. At the time, I didn't know if I would be capable of playing the part. It's a tough role. Not only do you have to play it, you have to live it, too. I had no experience.

There aren't many deaf actresses, so a hearing actress played Sarah in the Belgian production. The American film version was a huge success and Marlee Matlin won an Oscar for her performance. It was a tremendous responsibility to bring that role to life again.

After nine months of meeting with Jean, Sarah was born. We looked into each other's eyes. The more we saw each other, the more we discussed the part, the more I asked him questions about the character, the more patient he became, and the more interested I got. This time, I was the one who said, "I have to pass my exam first."

"Okay. But I need to know your answer before then. It's not easy producing a play like this."

Silence. Mouette was thinking.

I was attracted to him, the play, the part. Everything attracted me. Acting was what I loved. I would have never dared even hope for an offer like that. But I didn't want to be knocked off balance three months before my baccalaureate exam.

Dormant urges. Passionate desires in waiting. I had to achieve my goal all by myself.

"If you pass your exam, you'll play the part even better. But I know you're capable of playing the role." And he was serious, too!

Silent gaze. I like you. Silent gaze. We'll see each other again. Silent gaze. In three months.

Chapter 24

Mr. Implanter

One day, Marie and my mother were talking about a possible—but improbable—miracle operation that could make deaf people hear. They wondered if I would agree to such a thing.

"Marie, why do you say no? Maybe Emmanuelle would want to."

"That would surprise me! I know my sister better than anyone. She'd refuse for sure."

They batted the subject around for a while, then made a bet. Marie came up to me all excited to explain what the discussion was about. She was positive she was right.

She was. And she's still entirely right. Marie knows everything about me better than anyone. And on that topic, she could, in fact, answer for me.

I would refuse that type of operation. I consider it a form of ethnic cleansing. But whenever you use that expression, explanations are in order. I have a problem with my father on that point. He doesn't agree with my use of the term, or with my use of *purging*.

"Careful," he says. "Don't say something stupid."

But that's HIM. He's hearing. I'm ME. Mouette. I'm not talking racism when I use the term *purging*.

Those of us who are profoundly deaf from birth are a minority. We have our own culture and language. I cringe at doctors, researchers, or anyone else who wants to turn us into hearing people at all costs. It would destroy our identity to make us hearing. Wanting all children to be able to hear at birth is like wishing for a perfect world. It's like wanting all babies to be blond and blue-eyed.

So, no more Blacks? No more deaf people?

Why not just accept other people's imperfections? Everybody has them. In relation to you hearing people, Emmanuelle is imperfect. You think people have to be born with ears that hear and a mouth that talks. We all have to be identical. Just like the next guy in every detail. I like to compare myself to the Native American Indians. They were wiped out by the European and Christian civilizations. The Indians used a lot of signs to communicate, too. Hmm . . . interesting.

Other people hear. I don't. But I have my eyes. They're more observant than yours, naturally. I have hands that speak. A brain that stores information in its own way, according to my needs.

I'm not labeling hearing people imperfect. I refuse to do that. On the contrary, I would like to see the two communities come together in mutual respect. I give you my respect. I'm waiting for yours in return.

The world cannot and should not be perfect. Therein lies its wealth. Even if researchers succeed in localizing the gene responsible for children being born profoundly deaf like myself, even if they're able to fiddle with that gene, I reject the whole principle.

I can understand why adults who go deaf after having been able to hear seek help. It's because they suddenly become handicapped. They're deprived of a faculty they were used to, of their culture, their way of functioning, essentially of their *modus operandi.* But don't touch the children born like me, all the little seagulls of my flock the world over. Let them have the choice, the chance to find fulfillment in both cultures.

Deaf history is one of a long struggle. In 1620, a Spanish monk invented the rudiments of sign language. Later, in France, the Abbé de l'Épée expanded on them and founded an institute specializing in educating the deaf. Neither had any idea that the tremendous hope they had given the deaf world would at one point suddenly be snuffed out.

In the eighteenth century, the reputation of the institute in Paris was so great that King Louis XVI visited it to observe the teaching methods used there. They were revolutionary and all of Europe took an interest in them.

However, sign language was officially banned in the nineteenth century. *Mimicry,* as it was called, could no longer be used in schools. It was reviled because it was considered indecent and supposedly prevented the deaf from talking. It was labeled a "monkey language" and was spurned.

They forced children to articulate sounds they had never heard and never would. They essentially turned them into underdeveloped individuals. Doctors, educators, religious institutions, the entire hearing world united with incredible violence against us. Only the spoken word held sway.

It wasn't until January 1991, that the ban was lifted in France and parents could choose bilingualism for their children. That's an important option because it allows deaf children to have their own language, develop psychologically, and at the same time communicate with others in oral and written French. A whole century of what I call cultural terrorism by the hearing majority had gone by. It was insane! It was a dark century during which deaf people in Europe were deprived of the light of knowledge and had to acquiesce. Meanwhile, in the United States, sign language was considered a right and was on its way to becoming a veritable culture unto itself.

But today, with scientific and medical progress, and the invention of cochlear implants, the hegemony of the hearing over us has gone a step further. The implant is an infernal device that converts sound waves into electric currents. Platinum electrodes are placed inside the inner ear. A microprocessor is implanted under the scalp and the electrodes are linked to it by about fifteen relay channels. A tiny antenna, hidden behind the ear and connected to a small case, transmits sounds from the outside world to the processor. The microprocessor then encodes the sounds and retransmits them as signals to the auditory nerve. The individual wearing the device has to learn how to decode them.

Ever since the first operations of this type were performed in 1980, implants have been an issue in deaf communities around the world. Individuals like myself, who refuse the procedure, are looked upon as a handful of irresponsible activists with no understanding of science. Here's what people say about us:

"They're denouncing what they see as an attempt at ethnic cleansing of the deaf population. That's ridiculous."

Or else:

"Sign language is violent. It's not surprising that they reject us and that we reject them."

Or still:

"Sign language is antiquated and they want to turn it into empowerment!"

So who's talking about violence, empowerment, and rejection? I'm not, in any case. I refuse that surgical procedure because I'm an adult and it's my right to refuse it. On the other hand, three- or four-year-olds who have it forced on them don't have a say in the matter. I do. Usually I get pretty upset when I discuss this topic and it's quite obvious from the way I sign.

None of the doctors who tout the miraculousness of cochlear implants ever mention sign language. What they want is for deaf people to hear and speak like them. They claim we're just crying wolf. They consider us a "small group of activists who are being manipulated" and who are afraid that the "power" of sign language will disappear.

Not "power," Mr. Implant Surgeon. "Culture."

You don't talk about culture, gentleness, exchanges. You talk about surgery, the power of the scalpel, electrodes, encoded signals. Furthermore, you don't openly admit the damage this kind of surgery can cause.

You don't know everything about those electrodes, Mr. Implanter. They can break down in ten or twenty years. You don't have enough long-term evidence to be as conclusive as you are. You don't have the right to just do as you please.

You don't know what the individual tolerance threshold is for those encoded sounds. Adults complain about it. Little children can't adjust the device themselves or turn it off when it causes them pain. They have to suffer with it.

You provide positive data that's hard to challenge because we have no control over it. Your so-called *variable* results break down like this: 50% successful; 25% moderately successful, with a continued need to read lips after a long period of therapy and a confinement of the use of the device to low-noise environments (What progress!). And finally, 25% unsuccessful. This last group will never hear anything except unidentifiable noises and will end up permanently unplugging the implants. And you expect us to be satisfied with statistics like that? How about an impartial assessment?

What are all the three-year-olds in the 25% unsuccessful category supposed to do? Go see you in twenty years to protest? They won't have that option. You wouldn't be able to do anything for them at that point and you know it! The implant causes irreversible damage. Any chances of hearing that might have existed in a subject's cochlea before the operation are destroyed forever, regardless of age.

Noteworthy researchers are now talking about the generator potential of sound messages encoded on the auditory nerve as neural impulses. The function of those impulses is still unknown. When researchers finally crack the code, don't you think you'll look antiquated, too?

I'm sure you don't want to hear the story of the little girl who had a cochlear implant operation and then tearfully said, "There's a spider in my head."

Despite your intensive therapy after the implant, she couldn't decode sounds properly.

Haven't you heard about the woman who committed suicide three years after getting an implant because, psychologically and emotionally, she couldn't stand the new sounds entering her head from all directions?

I view implants as a form of rape. If adults agree to it, that's their business. But it frightens me when parents conspire with surgeons to impose that kind of rape on their children.

Your "electronic ear" frightens me, Mr. Implanter. You're going too far. Look at your professional code of ethics and reflect on it a little more. It should tell you something.

As usual, you wave the flag of science and progress. But you don't know anything about the deaf individuals you're talking about, their psychology, their acquired knowledge. You don't know anything about the future that lies ahead for the little deaf children you're trying to change.

Deaf people have attained a definite quality of life. They've adapted. Sign language has enabled them to develop fully. They speak, write, and conceptualize with the help of two different languages. Deaf children born to deaf parents have no alternative. And it's a fact that when an entire family is deaf, they live in a world that is completely different from yours. Accept it.

I have my own way of imagining all those sounds that permeate your world. To suddenly hear them would surely be disappointing, traumatizing, and even hellish. Conceive of the world differently from what my eyes tell me? Impossible. I would lose my identity, my sense of balance, my powers of imagination. I would lose myself. Sun-Coming-from-the-Heart would be lost in an unknown universe. I refuse to move to another planet.

Once a little girl asked me, shyly, "Why do they say it's good to put an implant in your head? Is it bad to be deaf?"

I often wonder if the whole thing isn't really a lobby movement orchestrated by implant manufacturers. There must be a lot of money in it if it's causing such a stir. The cost of an implant in France ranges from one hundred thousand to one hundred fifty thousand francs.

The world of noises, your noises, is unknown to me. And I don't miss it. I thank my family for having given me a silent culture. I speak and write French. I sign. Because of all that, I'm no longer just a seagull crying out without even being aware of it.

I think there's a strange resemblance between the implant and the devices the American military inserted in dolphins to try to decipher their language and perform experiments. Experiments . . .

For the last twenty years, which is about how old I am, some doctors, not all, have never stopped saying, "The deaf will be able to hear Beethoven!" At first, it was supposed to happen in the future, then the near future. Then they had to get private funding. After that, they said they wouldn't intervene in cases where deafness had existed for more than ten years. Then they decided to perform implant surgery on very young children, before their auditory brain cells atrophied. It was as if they had to act quickly, fast, before they could be proven wrong.

Ideas on the subject come and go. Information is incomplete and no one is sure of anything. Every case is unique and no one can swear that the operation will work for this or that deaf person. And to make things worse, they won't admit that they don't know.

I don't much like the idea of experimenting on human beings. I may not be a riled-up, round-the-clock activist, but I have a right to contradict what you're saying, Mr. Implanter.

My father and I took part in a public forum for the deaf, along with special education teachers, psychiatrists, lawmakers, and ear-nose-throat specialists. Our objective was to discuss the implant issue. At one point, a deaf girl started alluding to the deaf as a racial minority. Her parents were deaf. There were generations and generations of deaf people in her family. Not one of her relatives was hearing. Therefore she viewed deafness as a race unto itself. That's when my father got upset. He was shocked. He couldn't accept the way she was using the term. I had never seen him so mad.

"What does the word *race* mean? Are we going back to fascism? Do you want to claim the supremacy of the Aryan race? And what am I, then, in relation to my daughter? Do you mean to say I'm of a different race than my daughter? We belong to the same race!"

Then I spoke up and told the girl, "The word *race* doesn't strike me as at all appropriate to describe the deaf community."

"But why did your father get annoyed?"

"Listen. The sperm that gave me life was his sperm. It didn't come from a deaf person. The man who gave me life is hearing, not deaf. Deafness has nothing to do with race!"

She finally admitted I was right. It was the first time I saw my procreator in such a state of anger.

But we'll talk about implants again later, Dad. In both languages, because you accepted that I was different and you loved me enough to share that difference with me.

An implant surgeon could never be wrong? Who said that? Hippocrates?

Chapter 25

Taking Flight

arah, child of silence. Deaf Sarah, who refuses to speak. Violent, oppressed Sarah. Sensitive Sarah, in love. Desperate Sarah.

Two tremendous deaf actresses had played the role before me. Would I be able to carry it off? I thought about it constantly. And I studied and studied.

I finished the written part of my baccalaureate exam. Things were looking up. I was more afraid of the written test than the oral because it was hard to think and polish my sentences as fast as my pen would fly. I was more cut out for the oral. For a supposedly mute Mouette, that might seem strange. But that's how it is. I enjoy speaking more than writing.

I kept plugging away, preparing for the oral part of the exam. Philosophy was a problem in the beginning and I was a bit overwhelmed by it. I think it must be difficult for deaf students having trouble in school to express abstract concepts. I really had to work hard at it. I was already a little behind because I hadn't been applying myself. But I finally got into it. I was prepared to discuss the conscious, the subconscious, abstract notions, physical and verbal violence, truth and falsehood. I had been working so hard I looked like a sick seagull. Finish the exam, Laborit. They promised you the theater as a reward.

"Miss Laborit, tell me about the myth of the cave. Expand on . . ." That's how my oral exam started. With a question on Plato's concept of truth. It was hard, very hard. But I did it. The previous year, at my French oral, I explained to the examiner that I was deaf and asked for an interpreter. You would think I'd be allowed to have one. But it wasn't that easy. I had to fight for an interpreter, but I got one. I didn't want a teacher there by my side, or my mother, babying me. I wasn't going to be babied all my life. Life isn't like that. I didn't know the interpreter and he didn't know me. He was just there to translate what I said.

This time, the person testing me in philosophy was nice. He was intrigued by my situation and asked me a lot of questions about what I planned on doing later. I told him about the theater and he talked to me about art. He would have liked to have chatted longer, but we weren't there for that. So we moved on to the question. I started off with conviction.

Are the shadows in the cave reality or illusion, truth or falsehood? It's been two years since I took the exam, so I've forgotten some of what I said. In any event, I think I developed the topic well.

"The prisoners in the cave were deprived of natural light and therefore their vision was distorted in the light given off by a fire or candles. They saw shadows, only a distorted portion of things. Everything is an idea. Man must seek the truth of things. Natural light, sunlight, symbolizes that truth, that which is good and beautiful, etc."

Sun, truth. Light, truth. Oral exam, truth. I talked till my wrists and throat were sore.

After explaining the myth of the cave, Sun-Coming-from-the-Heart was exhausted. But she was rewarded with a good grade: 16 out of a possible 20 points in philosophy! Thanks to Plato and his sun.

I had passed my baccalaureate exam! And with a good grade, too! I was ready to spread my wings and fly to the theater. They were waiting for me.

There he was, Jean Dalric, my stage director/actor. Exchange of glances. Hello . . . hello. Hands that speak. The real work was about to begin.

Children of a Lesser God is about two worlds and the challenges of each: the world of James, who is hearing, and the world of Sarah, who is deaf. It's a story about rebellion, love, and humor.

Jean played James, a teacher at an institute for deaf students. James's teaching methods are unconventional. He wants to get the students out of their isolation, force them to read lips, and eventually speak.

Sarah refuses. Born deaf, she prefers to remain in her silent universe. She rejects the hearing world. He humiliates and hurts her. He has never tried to communicate with her. So why should she try to talk to him? Even her father has deserted her.

But Sarah ends up falling in love with James. In spite of her love for him, she tries to hold onto her identity and independence.

Exchange of glances: Sarah-James. Exchange of glances: Emmanuelle-Jean. Was Emmanuelle going to fall in love with Jean?

I was twenty years old. I had passed my baccalaureate exam. I was free to take flight and get emotionally involved with whatever or whomever I wanted. Including him. But I had to pass my test as an actress first.

Outside our theater company, no one believed the play would have a second run in France, not even the deaf. We had absolutely no financial or moral support. Jean was crazy. I love him. I also love his craziness.

I was learning a lot. Not only my role, but how to live with the other actors and actresses as a team. Confrontations. Arguments. Understanding. Love. Hearing and deaf people together. It was an extraordinary and priceless relationship of give and take. Like crystal. I appreciated Anie Balestra for her reliability, Nadine Basile for her affection and caring, Daniel Bremont for his gentleness, Joël Chalude, who is deaf, for his sense of humor, Jean Dalric for his strength and perseverance, Fanny Druilhe, who is also deaf, for her professionalism, and our sound effects engineer, Louis Amiel, for his good nature.

We went into rehearsal. The seagull was drowning between two waves, two stage directors, Levent Beskardes and Jean Dalric. One deaf, the other hearing. Drowning in the differences between their interpretation of the character and their stage directions. Mouette was panicking. Beskardes saw Sarah one way and Dalric, another. But the final decision to make Sarah become me or me become Sarah was mine.

Until then, I had thought the theater was paradise. Now it was becoming work. Real, professional work.

I kept asking questions. Why is Sarah so violent? Why is she so oppressed? Why does she want to wall herself up in her silence?

I worked very hard. I rehearsed my part over and over, but it still wasn't right. I would get upset and there were times when I said, "I'll never be able to do it! It's impossible!"

But I was getting better. Every once in a while, I would visualize the other two actresses who had played Sarah so well before me. Then I blotted them out so I wouldn't be distracted by other wavelengths. I was the one who had to feel Sarah and play her then and there. It was a tremendous opportunity and I couldn't let it slip by. Do it . . . Do it.

Sarah wasn't really me but rather my role as an actress. She wasn't me because she rejected the other world. She wasn't me because she was unhappy and refused to talk. She wasn't me because she carried the pain of exclusion, humiliation, and abandonment inside her.

The scene I had to work hardest on was the one where Sarah explains how her father deserted her when she was five. My father hadn't deserted me, so I had to really concentrate.

SARAH: On the last night, my father sat on the bed and cried. The next day, he left. My mother put a poster on the wall![1]

I just couldn't get it. I didn't know how to play it, how to get into character. She expresses so much pain in that memory and yet at the same time refuses to show it. She hides behind painful irony and doesn't want to talk about it. Then, all of a sudden, the memory resurfaces and shows on her face!

How could I bring subtlety to her suffering? I tried to think of personal memories that best paralleled her anguish, but I didn't have any that approached it. I couldn't simply sign that my father had deserted me, burst into tears, and consider the scene done! I needed to feel true, subtle emotion. I needed to suffer as I signed her suffering. And to keep it in check with the closing line: "My mother put a poster on the wall!"

The last thing Sarah wants to do is show emotion. She especially doesn't want to cry. She can't. But everything she's hiding and desperately holding back inside her has to be seen on her face. On my face. I rehearsed the scene for a long time with Jean. I almost quit because of it. Then it came to me, like a ray of light.

After a month and a half of rehearsal, it was opening night. My whole family was there. So was Chantal Liennel, who had played the part ten years earlier in the first French production.

I had real stage fright. A fear I can't quite describe and that wouldn't leave me from beginning to end. My heart was beating wildly. Pounding. I

---

[1] Translators' note: This is an excerpt from the French adaptation of Mark Medoff's *Children of a Lesser God*. In the scene in question, Medoff's original text is slightly different. It reads as follows: "My father stayed with me that night. He cried. I never saw him again . . . After he left, my mother put a picture of the Virgin Mary on the wall."

felt out of breath, like my legs were going to give way. My description is rather condensed. Actually, it was worse than that. Words can't describe it.

I was in a fog the whole time I was acting. I was somewhere else. I didn't see anything. I didn't feel the presence of the audience. I was lost onstage, completely submerged in my role. My mind was on nothing else.

When the curtain came down and I finally started breathing again, I wanted to burst into tears. Tears of joy. But I held them back and took my bows.

I had done it! Me, all alone. I had succeeded! I had played the part from start to finish! I hadn't passed out or forgotten my lines. I hadn't tripped on the curtain. And my heart hadn't stopped beating from fear.

I didn't even see the audience's reaction. My mind was still muddled. I had only one thought: I had done it.

Marie came running up in tears to give me flowers. That's when I broke down. I cried with her. We cried in each other's arms. The emotion was enormous. Infinite joy.

Over the next few days, my head was more together. I realized I was incapable of using audience feedback to pace my acting. Jean could hear the audience, but I couldn't. He could adapt his acting to the audience's laughter and whispers of emotion. He would pause to "listen" and act as if the pauses were part of the play. I had to find a strategy, another way to get my cues. I couldn't rely solely on his reactions, his face, how he acted the part differently depending on whether the audience was laughing or crying.

Find a way, Emmanuelle. Learn your trade. Be a deaf actress. You're an actress riding the wave of a silent audience. Listen, Mouette. Listen with your entire body to the music of the audience, its rhythm, its laughter, its emotion. You have to perceive it. Listen with your whole being.

I found a way! It was fabulous. I was finally able to feel the positive and negative vibrations, the warmth or coldness of the audience. I had just discovered something that defies explanation either in writing or sign language. It's beyond words, phrases, sounds. Maybe it's a kind of mysterious osmosis. I have no idea, but I had found it. It was mine!

Mother was proud of me: "Did you know I wanted to name you Sarah when you were born? But your grandmother didn't want me to."

Emmanuelle was playing Sarah. I'm sure it wasn't just a matter of chance. Was it a sign?

I knew the critics weren't going to be easy on me, but the reviews were fantastic. Thank you for recognizing my talent as an actress. Theater and film professionals, who are sensitive to everything related to the voice as a channel for human emotions, had recognized something in my performance that experts on deafness persist in rejecting. Night after night, we played to enthusiastic Paris audiences at the *Théâtre Mouffetard* and later the *Théâtre du Ranelagh*. The father of a deaf child told me that, after seeing the play, he decided to learn sign language for his daughter. Until then, he had categorically refused. But when he saw the play, he said it made him understand and he cried. I cried, too.

We were forging ahead, taking flight, going ever further, and playing to more and more audiences. We were riding along on the crests of success . . . and love. I was no longer "I." I had become "we."

The play was nominated for a Molière award in more than one category.

I read in the paper that Emmanuelle Laborit had been nominated for a Molière in the category of best new talent for 1993. Jean had been nominated for best play adaptation.

Our eyes met. Jean said to me, tenderly, "You have to be just as prepared to win as to lose. Just be ready. Ready."

My take-off had been so quick, I was still in the air. So I prepared myself for both eventualities, of course with a preference for the first! I kept thinking in the back of my mind that winning a Molière award would be absolutely wonderful. I was sure that kind of joy gave you goose bumps. Happiness pervaded your entire body. So many kinds of happiness were coming my way all at once.

Stop dreaming, Emmanuelle. Keep your feet on the ground. Be ready.

Chapter 26
Seagull in Suspense

I t's very hard for me to express in writing the emotion and happiness I felt in this chapter of my life. I experienced those emotions physically and can express them so much better in sign.

It took a whole day to get ready. There was the dress, getting my hair done, the makeup. Mouette was all dressed up in an evening gown, ready for the ball.

There were a lot of talented people in the running for Molière awards. Professional actors. I was the only deaf person.

On awards night, my parents were somewhere on one side of the theater, my sister was on the other, and the *Children of a Lesser God* cast members were scattered about in the audience. I would have preferred to have my little family close to me. My real family and my adopted family, all together.

I was with Jean. He smiled at me and held my hand. He was nervous, too. Would he get a Molière? Would I? Would neither of us?

We looked at each other. We loved each other.

I had butterflies in my stomach. I was so scared I couldn't see what was going on around me. I was prepared to lose. That night, losing was more on my mind than winning. The TV cameras, the lights, the cameras flashing, the excitement, the tension in the air. The theater was packed. All those famous, stunningly beautiful actresses and all those actors were used to ceremonies like that. Newcomers to the circle of pros feel like kids thrown in the water to learn how to swim. Thrown into an ocean of staring eyes, a tide of faces, and rows of hands. All the mouths talking to each other around me knew things I didn't yet. They knew how to look confident, how to speak and critique with self-assurance.

I had my interpreter, Dominique Hof—the one I've always had. She knows me like a book. She can guess what I want to say from my very first sign. I had Jean, too. His love on and offstage had become a beacon for me. He signed, "Is everything okay? Do you feel all right?"

I really didn't, but I said yes!

I didn't want to just go up on stage in front of that distinguished audience, cry, say thank you, and leave like a robot. I wanted to be able to say something to them. I was at least sure of that. But if I didn't win, I wanted to be able to sit among them and control myself. Accept defeat graciously. The theater world was like a third home to me. It had opened its doors and I had to show I was worthy of the welcome.

As a teenager, I used to dream about Marilyn Monroe. She was so fragile in the face of the emotional demands of her profession. I put pictures of her everywhere. I wasn't Marilyn Monroe and this wasn't Hollywood, but for me it was all the same. This was the first time a deaf actress had been nominated for a Molière award. It was a first, and it had fallen to me. Even if I didn't get it, I had already made it over a major hurdle.

In the next few minutes one of two emotions would come over me: I'd either be whisked to the stage or held to my seat. The magnificent actress Edwige Feuillere was onstage along with Stephane Freiss, who had won the Molière for best new talent the year before. Jean signed to me that they were starting to announce the five nominees in my category.

I couldn't stand it any longer. I wanted to know in a split second. Quick, quick. So my hands would stop shaking, so that . . . so it would be over.

They ripped open the envelope. If I won, the interpreter would let me know. They came to get her when they started reading off the names and told her to be ready to go up on stage in the event that . . . Since they did that, maybe it meant . . .

But Jean heard it first. He heard the "Em" of Emmanuelle and was already standing before the interpreter had time to finish signing to me. He knew. Em . . . it had to be me.

I didn't know who to look at. Him? The interpreter? The stage?

I got up in a daze. Our eyes met. No need to speak. I started walking to the stage, wobbling the whole way. A million things with no logical connection were running through my mind. A flood of images. Without re-alizing it, I was already signing. As I walked down the aisle, I was thinking of what I should say. It seemed like an endlessly long walk to the stage. My legs were shaking and I was afraid of falling. My dress, my incredibly high heels; I wasn't used to walking in them and was sure I was going to fall flat on my face. Walking on those stilts, I had to really concentrate. I saw my mother, waved to my father, looked at my feet and went over what I was going to say. I looked at my feet again. I couldn't stop looking at them. I was careful to watch where my feet were going. I went up the stairs and at that point could finally look up. I had made it.

Edwige Feuillere was far, far away onstage, smiling and waiting for me. She was waiting for *me!*

Suddenly, I saw the audience in front of me. So many people! I couldn't walk straight. I was all choked up. My throat was in a knot and my emotions were about to burst forth. I didn't want to cry, I really didn't, but I felt it coming. It overpowered me and just came out.

I was crying as I walked up to that *grande dame* of the theater, waiting for me with open arms. I tensed up and was sure I wouldn't be able to express myself in sign language. It wasn't coming. I clumsily signed "thank you." My gears were stuck and everything was a blur.

Then, a little voice in my head said, "Come on Emmanuelle! The au-dience is out there! The Molière awards audience. Go on! Say something!"

I put my fears and emotions aside and began. "Thank you, thank you, thank you."

I felt a little better. I continued with my speech, holding my emo-tion back, desperately trying to contain it. I had promised myself that I would say what I wanted without losing my nerve.

"It's hard for me to sign. This is the first time a deaf person has been recognized as a professional actor and received a Molière award. I'm so happy for deaf people everywhere. Please excuse me. I'm very moved. I have real tears in my eyes. I'd like to teach you a very easy and beautiful sign . . . I'd like for you to do it with me . . ."

I made the sign for "united." It's such a beautiful sign. I love it so much. It's the one on the poster for *Children of a Lesser God*.

I waited for everybody to make the sign but no one did. I was panic-stricken. No one was moving. I thought to myself, "What's the point of trying to communicate? No one feels the same emotion that I do."

I felt ridiculous. It was horrible. I turned to the interpreter and she quickly explained to me that in interpreting there is always a time lag. That explained the interminable pause when nothing was happening! It was the time it took to translate my speech! I was so flustered I hadn't even thought about that. I made the sign again and all of a sudden I saw one person, then several more, and finally the whole audience doing it! Their arms raised, their hands in the shape of butterflies as their fingers made the sign for unity.

It was the most beautiful gift in the world—all those people in front of me, making the same sign. To thank them, I said orally, "I love you."

I had lost my voice because of the emotion and I know only a few people probably heard what the voiceless seagull murmured.

I kissed Edwige Feuillere and ran backstage. My sister rushed down the aisle and threw herself into my arms.

I still hadn't fully realized that I had been awarded the Molière for best new talent of 1993. I was blinded by the flashes from the cameras. It was terrible. Ten whole minutes of machinegun-like flashes.

Then it was Jean's turn to go up on stage. Molière for best play adaptation.

We had both won. Happiness here we come.

Chapter 27

Good-bye

Not too long ago, I came across the famous Proust questionnaire. Two of the questions are: What is your favorite saying? What natural gift would you like to possess? My answer to the first is: Live life to the fullest. As for the second, I already have the gift I want—I'm deaf.

The day after the Molière awards ceremony, all the newspapers printed more or less the same headline: "Deaf-Mute Wins Molière Award."

Not Emmanuelle Laborit, but "deaf-mute." "Emmanuelle Laborit" appeared in fine print, under the picture.

I'm always surprised by the term *deaf-mute*. Mute means unable to speak. People see me as someone who can't speak! That's ridiculous. I can. With my hands as well as my mouth. I speak in sign and French. Using sign language doesn't mean you're mute. I can speak, yell, laugh, and cry. Sounds come out of my mouth. Nobody cut my tongue out. My voice is different, that's all.

I never told journalists that I couldn't speak. It's just that my sign language vocabulary is broader and so it's easier for me to answer their questions using sign, with an interpreter.

Anecdote: After all the articles that came out about me in the press, a speech therapy teacher criticized me, saying I should have spoken to the journalists orally instead of using sign. She told me it was my fault if people thought the deaf were mute! She accused me of lying. In her opinion, I had become the spokesperson for the deaf population and I should assume that responsibility by suing the journalists who used the word *mute!* A lawsuit over one word. How ridiculous!

That teacher's job is to "de-mute" deaf people, to make them talk. So naturally, for her, sign language is a sublanguage, something miserably inferior, a code incapable of conveying abstract concepts. Just visual images!

That so-called deaf specialist hasn't understood a thing about the deaf. It's too bad for her, but it's even worse for them.

Goethe once said there's nothing more frightening than ignorance in action. And since we're talking about the theater, let me assume the role of Molière's character, Dorante, for a moment to say, "I would like to know if the greatest rule of all is not to please, and if a play has attained that goal, has it not followed the right path?"

I can say that in sign language, too.

Thank you, Monsieur Molière.

It was wild. Journalists, interviews, photos, Cannes, my beautiful white dress, walking up the staircase, all those people who had forgotten I couldn't hear calling out to me. It was beautiful. Sheer happiness. But it was murder, too.

I was asked to appear on TV shows. I made the rounds to all the stations and started getting offers for movie parts. Everything was going so fast, I was in a whirlwind. And the whole time, we were touring France with *Children of a Lesser God*. Every night, I trembled as I took my bows and saw all the hands in the audience raised high in applause. I could "hear" success. It vibrated throughout my body.

Jean has made me work hard. He loves me. We've gone forward, hand in hand. He's my hearing point of reference. My sign language companion and traveling partner in life's journey.

The little red light on my phone never stops blinking. There are so many projects in Mouette's life now. So many things to do, to say, to perform. To love.

I'm proud and happy that, because of me, the media have taken an interest in the world of silence. They're so uninformed about the deaf. All the journalists I meet give me the impression they're just discovering we exist. They're nice, sweet, enthusiastic, attentive, even admiring. That's really positive.

But some questions make me hit the ceiling. There's one in particular that they ask over and over again: "What's your silence like? Is it quieter than the silence in a cave or underwater?"

A cave? Caves aren't silent as far as I'm concerned. They're full of smells. They're damp. Caves are teaming with the noise of sensations. Underwater? I'm right at home down there. I'm an underwater seagull who loves diving. Underwater, I'm just like you. And I'm an above water seagull who loves the sun and sea, too.

My silence and yours aren't the same. Mine would be more akin to having my eyes shut, my hands paralyzed, my body numb to sensation, my skin unresponsive. It would be more like a physical silence.

Sometimes, when I'm being interviewed, I feel like saying that I'm not really crazy about expressions such as *hearing-impaired* and *hearing deficient*. When the deaf refer to themselves, they use the word *deaf*. It's very clear. But *hearing-impaired?* Is it really a case of impairment? Should we call other people *hearing-unimpaired?*

One last question: "Are you planning to have children?"

Answer: Yes.

Follow-up question: "Would you want them to be deaf or hearing?"

Answer: They'll be whatever they are. They'll be my children. Period.

For the time being, that's still in the planning stage. But, whether deaf or hearing, my child will be bilingual and know both worlds, as I do. If deaf, my child will learn sign language very early, and, at the same time, be exposed to French. If I have a hearing child, I'll respect his or her natural language and he or she will learn mine. My child will hear my voice and get used to it. The way my mother, sister, and father did. My child will hear me. I'll be a mother seagull.

Then I'll be a mother seagull a second time. Having a brother or sister is important. I want my children to learn how to quarrel, how to do things for themselves, how to share, how to love each other. Like my sister and I did. And later on, I'll become a grandmother seagull.

Once when I was little, my maternal grandmother, who's very religious, told me a story. I loved it when she told me stories. That day, she told me *my* story, and I'll never forget it. She said, "You know, you were chosen by God. He decided that you'd be deaf, because he wanted you to give something to other people . . . hearing people. If you were hearing, you might not amount to anything special. You'd just be an ordinary little girl, incapable of bringing anything unique to others. But he chose to make you deaf so that you could bring something to the world."

I didn't quite know who or what God was. I didn't have any religious training because my parents were opposed to it. My mother had suffered because of hers. But to hear Grandmother talk about God, you'd think she knew him personally. She spoke with real conviction. He had chosen to make me deaf. I was going to bring something to the world. It was Grandmother who gave me a kind of philosophy of life. She gave me strength. Determination.

But I'm the one who pushes myself, Grandmother. I don't get my strength from God, but from myself.

I do feel there's a spirit somewhere, something beyond us, but I don't know if it's God. For me, it has no name. It's a superior force. Sometimes I talk to it. When I want something very badly, like to succeed, achieve a goal, excel, or not to be afraid, I talk to it as if to a person. To myself, perhaps, or to someone who might take care of me. It's actually an inner dialog.

Mouette, the resolute seagull, says, "Stop being afraid. Don't be nervous. You can do it. Go on! Go for it!"

Then another voice, the voice of Mouette, the philosophical seagull, answers, "See? Everything's going fine. You aren't afraid or nervous. You're doing it. Everything's great. You did it!"

True, I'm only twenty-two, so I've only had those kinds of discussions with myself (or with myself and the other force) about things that are typical of someone my age. For example:

"Stop doing dumb things. Face life straight on."

"Finish school. You'll pass your exam. Don't be scared."

"Go on stage. Work at it. You'll get Sarah's part right."

That's how I've pondered the problems, both big and small, of my young life. There have been ups and downs. There have been times when I felt more isolated, more alone, than usual and others when I felt less so.

I still have a lot to learn, and I ask myself a lot of questions. Learning is a lifelong activity. If you stop learning, you're done for. Life goes on, day after day. There are always surprises and different things to learn. That's how you really enjoy life to the fullest. Fighting is my philosophy. You have to fight to live. Do everything, get involved, and never slack off. Simple pleasures are important, too. You need to grab the little everyday joys and hold onto them.

Sometimes I have doubts. Is the progress report on my life up to now good or bad? Have I accomplished anything important?

I'm not very old, but an incredible amount of things have happened to me since my birth. I've aged in high gear. I experimented with things early, too early. I feel like I grew up very fast and haven't yet taken the time to go back and assess the road I've traveled. Somebody once asked me, "Do you mean to say that, when you were seven, you already had an image of who you were? You were already talking about your soul?"

Yes, I had to, because before the age of seven I had nothing. Then, all of a sudden, I was able to communicate. I forged an identity, an image of myself, very quickly. Maybe it was to make up for lost time. At thirteen, I felt like an adult. But now that I'm twenty-two, I know I still have a ways to go.

I need other people, dialog, a community. I couldn't live without the hearing and I couldn't live without the deaf, either. Communicating is a passion of mine.

Sometimes I need breathing space in one world or the other. I need to stand on the sidelines and fold my wings. But not for too long.

I need to communicate. If I couldn't, I would yell, I would bang on things, I would let the whole world know. I would feel all alone on the planet.

My grandmother's story is starting to come true. I'm giving my all to the hearing and deaf worlds: my words and my heart, my will to communicate and bring the two worlds together. With all my heart.

I'm a seagull who loves the theater and life; who loves both worlds: the one that belongs to the children of silence and the one that belongs to the children of sound. I'm a seagull who can fly over both, equally content to land in either. I can speak out for those who aren't fortunate enough to be able to do it for themselves. I can listen to people, talk to them, and understand them.

A while back, when I began the difficult task of writing this book, it made me tremble with apprehension. But I wanted to do it because writing is important to me. It's a form of communication that I hadn't attempted with any degree of seriousness yet.

Hearing people write books about the deaf. Jean Gremion, a philosophy professor, journalist, and theater expert spent several years studying the deaf world and wrote a fabulous book called *La Planète des sourds* (*The Planet of the Deaf*). In it, he makes the following point: The hearing have everything to learn from people who speak with their bodies. The richness of their gestural language is one of the treasures of humanity.

I don't know of any books written by deaf people in France, or Europe for that matter. Some people told me I wouldn't be able to do it.

But I wanted to make it happen with all my heart, as much to speak to myself as to deaf and hearing people. I wanted to give the most candid account possible of my life so far.

I especially wanted to do it in your native language. The language of my parents. My adopted language.

> The seagull has grown up and flies with her own wings.
> I see just as I might hear.
> My eyes are my ears.
> I can write as well as sign.
> My hands speak two languages.
> I offer my difference to you.
> My heart is deaf to nothing in this double world.
> It's very hard for me to leave you.

Emmanuelle Laborit

Spring 1994